A Naturalist's Years *in the* Rocky Mountains

A Naturalist's Years *in the* Rocky Mountains

HOWARD ENSIGN EVANS

JOHNSON BOOKS

AN IMPRINT OF BOWER HOUSE

DENVER

Designed by Margaret McCullough
Photography by Howard Ensign Evans

Library of Congress Cataloging-in-Publication Data
Evans, Howard Ensign
  A naturalist's years in the Rocky Mountains \ Howard Ensign Evans.
     p.   cm.
  Includes bibliographical references (p.)
  ISBN 978-1-55566-310-0
  i. Animal behavior—Colorado. 2. Animal behavior—Rocky Mountains.
  I. Title.

QL751.6 .E925 2001   00-054961
591.753'0978—dc21

Contents

Contents

I

Life on a Granite Cliff

FOR THIRTEEN YEARS my wife and I lived in a home on the edge of a granite cliff overlooking a broad panorama of hills and valleys, culminating in the Mummy Range, one of the few east-west ranges in the predominately north-south bearing Rocky Mountains. At seventy-eight hundred feet elevation, we could look down into the valley of the Cache la Poudre River, a thousand feet below, and on to the crests of the Mummies, well over twelve thousand feet high and always bearing at least a little snow all through the summer. Our house was backed by groves of ponderosa pines and Douglas-firs, a wild place, especially when assailed by raw winds from the high country, or when snow was piled high in winter or skies were pierced by lightning in summer. Wild, too, in terms mammalian, avian, or insectan. These were the best of friends, surviving the vagaries of the weather with us, tolerating us even though we had usurped a piece of their habitat.

The passage of time is something even our vaunted technology can do nothing about, nor can it erase time's ravages on the human body and mind. So we have left our aerie and moved to the city, no longer able to chop wood and shovel snow well enough to survive another winter. But we have not left it in spirit. Over the years we came to know our wild neighbors well, and we shall remember them even though they have no doubt scarcely noticed our disappearance. Such was the diversity of life that surrounded us that we were constantly discovering neighbors we didn't know we had—or trying to become better acquainted with the most familiar. Often this led us to books for answers. Books often helped with the larger creatures, but for lesser forms of life we were often on our own. So we spent a good deal of effort trying to fathom the lives of some of the insects that shared our living space.

First, a few words about our mountain home. Our deck and windows overlooked a tumble of lichen-covered boulders, interrupted here and there by currant, thimbleberry, and waxflower (*Jamesia*) bushes and a few small junipers and pines. In early summer there were yellow splashes of ragworts, blue splashes of penstemons, and an occasional scarlet Indian paintbrush among the rocks. Over time, many of the resident mammals passed in review there: marmots, golden-mantled ground squirrels, chipmunks, rabbits, squirrels, now and then a long-tailed weasel or a bobcat. The meadows below were traversed by mule deer and now and then by a herd of elk. Once a black bear came onto our deck and left a dirty paw print on our window, and once after a snow storm a mountain lion left a trail of tracks around our house. For a time, spotted skunks lived under the house, and each fall woodrats were unwelcome guests there. Coyotes howled on distant hillsides.

Hawks rode the updrafts along the cliffs, often leaving us somewhat frustrated, since our field guides showed hawks from the underside, while we looked down on them. Golden eagles sometimes perched on a dead tree not far below our deck, and at night owls and poorwills made their presence known. Once we saw a goshawk snatch a chipmunk from a stump, and another time a goshawk tried without success to take a squirrel from our deck, spreading his banded tail as he braked to avoid hitting the house. Several times we watched male blue grouse booming from the branch of a pine, and now and then we intercepted female grouse with their chicks.

Our calendar was no longer filled with appointments for committee meetings but with appointments with wildlife. We could anticipate the first mountain bluebirds in late February or early March, and about the same time the first flowers, spring beauties (*Claytonia*). Early April would see the first turkey vultures and white-throated swifts traversing the air space beyond our deck, and the first chipmunks, ground squirrels, and marmots would be out and about. Pasque flowers and sand lilies would soon be in bloom, and a few butterflies on the wing. Early May would see the return of the broad-tailed hummingbirds, house wrens, yellow-rumped warblers, and green-tailed towhees. A rock wren would be singing his irrepressible medley from a boulder. Fleabanes, saxifrage, creeping phlox, and wallflowers would be in bloom. By mid-May there would be golden banner, blue-flag iris, and other wildflowers to admire. In early June, the nighthawks would finally be back, and miners' candles (*Cryptantha*) blooming on hillsides. Those flashes of the tropics, western tanagers, would sing from the treetops. So much to take in!

The warmer months were filled with the hum of insects. Two kinds of cicadas added their more mechanical songs to those of birds, one a "clicker," the other a "buzzer." Fortunately there were no mosquitoes to hound us when we slept on the deck. Wood ticks (not really insects) were a bother when we were hiking, necessitating a deticking episode when we returned. Spruce budworms sometimes picked on our Douglas-firs, mountain pine beetles on our ponderosas. Ants sometimes invaded the kitchen. But by and large we had little cause to complain, and much to study and enjoy, in the fullness of the local insect fauna.

In summer there were squaw currants and chokecherries to be harvested, and jellies and wines to be made. Puffball mushrooms sprang up after rains and proved delicious when fried in butter. There were rainbow trout in nearby ponds and brown trout in local streams (neither native to the area). We lived as lightly on the land as we were able. One year we tried to grow a garden, but in spite of our fences the deer and ground squirrels nibbled off the plants as fast as they grew. We composted our food wastes and did not object to magpies scavenging for whatever they could find that was edible.

When the rabbit brush began to bloom it was time for the nighthawks and hummingbirds to head south, and fresh snows began to collect on the high peaks. The silvery tags on the seeds of mountain mahogany bushes began to brighten the hillsides, and aspens to turn gold.

Even winter had its rewards. Our seed feeders became crowded with mountain chickadees, Steller's jays, Cassin's finches, pine siskins, and nuthatches of three species. On snowy winter days, gray-capped rosy finches descended to our deck in numbers. Tassel-eared squirrels visited our feeders regularly, pine squirrels once in a while, and once, for a few days, a rock squirrel. Once a weasel in his white winter garb came to our suet feeder and let us approach him closely (another time a raccoon carried the whole feeder away). In very early spring small, black, wingless scorpion flies (*Boreus*) appeared on snowdrifts, apparently preferring that strange habitat to summer's largess. As spring progressed, our birdhouses became filled with bluebirds, house wrens, now and then chickadees, nuthatches, or violet-green swallows.

Our home was in what is often called the Transition Zone, transitional between the more humid high mountains and the semiarid foothills and plains. Looking south from our house we could scan the higher altitude forests, with their lodgepole pines, Engelmann spruce, and subalpine firs. Here and there were patches of aspens and, yes, rather frequent clear-cuts. Above the forests was alpine tundra, from this distance seemingly empty except for whatever snow it held seasonally. We knew the tundra was not really empty, but in summer clothed with alpine flowers and harboring pipits, pikas, and other wildlife. The high forests were similarly rich in wildlife: gray jays, pine squirrels, snowshoe hares, blue columbine, fairy slipper orchids, and much more. Knowing something of the inhabitants of each zone, we could visit them vicariously at any time (and personally, once in a while). Two areas designated as wilderness were visible from our windows, parts of Rocky Mountain National Park, and the gorges of a wild and scenic river, the Cache la Poudre. Over time, we came to know the river so well that we wrote a book about its natural history.

Three times we witnessed forest fires from our house, one of them close enough that we were asked to evacuate. When the wind shifted and blew the fire back on itself, the next day, we were able to return. Lightning-caused forest fires must have occurred here for centuries, and the forests may be the better for them. But now that many people have built their houses in the mountains (as we did), the fires must be extinguished as quickly as possible. A forest fire is a fearsome thing to watch, even from a distance, and one cannot help mourning the sudden death of trees and their attending wildlife.

Looking east from our house, we could see a tumble of foothills and a broad stretch of plains, where we knew hawks hunted prairie dogs and lark buntings floated their arias above the buffalo grass. Perhaps the richness of life we could embrace from our aerie did not rival a tropical rainforest, but in terms of diversity of life styles, with respect to environmental variables, it could hardly have been surpassed.

We should say a bit about ourselves. Mary Alice and I had been married for thirty-two years when we moved to the mountains, both of us former teachers of various biological topics at several institutions. We once believed that no occupation was more fundamental to human society than teaching, and that no topic was more worth pursuing than the study of life itself, in all its diversity. On our better days we still believe it.

It has been three years since we left our mountain home. How bright the stars were there! Lying in our sleeping bags on our deck, we could watch the ceiling of stars spin about the north star, a cosmic carousel bearing Cassiopeia, Perseus, and other ghostly Greeks. Focusing on one star, we fancied we could feel the slow rotation of the earth. Orion seemed a reliable neighbor—the planets friends that came and went as they pleased. The chirping of crickets provided just the right accompaniment.

Here in the city the stars are fewer and more dimly lit. Of course the reason is the competition of city lights and the diffuse cloud of chemicals through which they shine. House sparrows have taken the place of Cassin's finches, and the black birds we see are crows rather than ravens. Fields of leafy spurge and other weedy, alien plants fill spaces not covered with asphalt. It is not hard to picture a time when the earth's fauna and flora will be made up of the same people-friendly plants and animals everywhere. The twenty-first century will be a time for saying goodbye (if we care that much) to species that cannot adjust themselves to our way of life. We ourselves will not see much of the twenty-first century, but our children and grandchildren will. We might have left them a world in which birdsong could be heard above the roar of machines, where one could smell the fragrance of a forest inviolate. Instead we left them to be haunted by the sights and sounds of a natural world that is retreating, one day beyond recall.

2

Thatcher Ants

ON BRIGHT SUMMER DAYS it is good to simply wander about aimlessly, eyes on the ground, trying to avoid stepping on the wildflowers and mushrooms, startling grasshoppers from the grass and rabbits from the bushes. The patterns of nature's carpet are endless and never repeated, neither in space nor time. Images pass before one's eyes and are quickly gone. One can only revel in the moment, alert to every detail and aware that each moment is fleeting, each pattern never to be repeated precisely.

Sometimes there are images so striking that one is impelled to recapture them. When shooting star primroses painted pink a mossy bank in a nearby ravine, we returned almost daily to enjoy them. A local giant puffball mushroom grew to such a size (approximating a basketball) that we returned almost daily to measure it. And some of the goings-on in local meadows and woodlands were so notable that we simply sat and watched.

Such are the colonies of thatcher ants that were scattered about on local hillsides. These are the most admirable of ants; they are handsome (as ants go) and, unlike some ants, have no sting and little propensity to bite. Although the nearest colony was only about a hundred feet from our house, thatcher ants never invaded our kitchen (although three other kinds did so, sometimes in numbers). Each summer day, except during rain or hot, direct sunlight, they milled about on the thatched roofs of their homes, forever moving about sticks, needles of pines and Douglas-firs, scales of pine cones, rodent droppings, and small pebbles. Often they seemed to do nothing but rush about, as if looking for something useful to do. The word "redundancy" comes to mind: there seemed to be more ants than there were things to keep them busy.

Each ant is bicolored, like a sports car. The head and thorax are orange-brown, the abdomen black with a sheen of short, silvery pubescence. The legs are black, hence the scientific name applied long ago by Swiss myrmecologist and psychologist Auguste Forel, *Formica obscuripes* (Latin for ant with dark feet). Now and then an ant appears on the nest sporting a bright orange head and thorax. No doubt these are workers that have recently emerged from their cocoons and will soon darken to the usual color. Sometimes an ant appears that is smaller than the others and entirely black. These ants measure about three-sixteenths of an inch in length and have a head only slightly wider than the thorax. In contrast, most of the ants measure about a quarter of an inch and have heads considerably wider than their thoraces.

The colony nearest our house had a dome-shaped mound about three feet across and one and a half feet high in the middle. It was built at the base of a spreading, partially dead bitterbrush. Another nest, a quarter of a mile away, was pyramidal, built against a fallen tree trunk. Both were in open woodland but exposed to morning sunlight. Both nests had no openings at night, in bad weather, or in hot, direct sunshine. But by mid-morning, on pleasant days, there would be twenty or more openings, an inch or so across, where ants moved in and out. These ants do not "thatch" in the manner of thatch-roofed houses of some parts of the world. The twigs, needles, and what-not are piled at random on the roof. Yet the ants pull them about as it they had some grand design in mind. Indeed they are ful-filling an important (if wholly genetically determined) objective, for the mound they are building will act as a compost heap, raising the temperature within and helping the larvae develop more rapidly.

Thatcher ants have intrigued curious people for many years. Over half a century ago a biologist of our acquaintance, Neal Weber, wrote a long report about them in *Ecological Monographs*. Weber spent much of his life at Swarthmore College, and whenever free from teaching devoted his life to the study of ants. Unlike us, he did not hesitate to dig up nests to study their inner structure. He found that the thatching extends down to a depth of ten inches, more or less, and on average may measure nearly a bushel. Chambers in which brood is reared occur to a depth of about four feet. He estimated colony size to vary from about nineteen thousand individuals to at least twice that many.

Weber reported that reproductives (winged males and females) swarm from the nest in summer. Mary Talbot, working in Michigan, reported that swarming occurs there in June. Winged females, she found, leave the nest and gather on grasses or bushes in a "swarm area," which may be reused over several days and even used a subsequent season. Males fly to the area and seek out the females. Sometimes several males try to mate with the same female, producing a tight ball of struggling ants. Since members of several colonies may use the same swarm area, there is a lessened chance that males will mate with sisters.

We mention these observations of Mary Talbot since in fact we never observed a mating flight in our area. Rather, over several days in May, we saw a few winged males and females emerge from the nest and walk about, the males sometimes climbing up sticks and taking flight weakly. The workers seemed to ignore the males but took great interest

in the females. Each female (a potential queen) was surrounded by workers, who pulled her about and in at least
some cases injured or even killed her. We did not understand this behavior. Perhaps it was simply not time to
swarm, and the few individuals that emerged with wings
were simply eliminated. We assume that, as in most social
insects, castes are determined by the underfeeding or over-
feeding of larvae by the workers, in response to cues indicating the need for members of a particular caste. In so large
a colony, it may be that some messages are misdirected or
ambiguous. At least it was food for thought while we
watched the traffic on a local ant mound.

Other events did occur besides the endless milling about
and rearranging of thatch. Now and then a worker carried
off a dead ant or an empty cocoon and deposited it away
from the nest. Other ants arrived carrying dead insects: ear-
wigs, beetles, small caterpillars, grasshoppers, and so forth.
Most of these were probably found dead, although some
may have been killed. Neal Weber published a two-page-
long list of plunder taken by the ants in his study area. These
insects provide the major source of protein for the develop-
ing larvae. Other workers are off on local trees and bushes
exploiting a source of carbohydrates: the honeydew secreted
by aphids, leafhoppers, and other sucking insects. Thatcher
ants are also known to attend the larvae of lycaenid butterflies ("blues"), where they feed on the sweet secretions of
those larvae and also protect them from parasites.

Still another source of food, in season, is provided by the
black seeds of mountain ball cacti, which abounded in our
area and were adorned with welcome pink blossoms in
May. Each blossom produces a seed with a small mass of
protein attached. The ants harvest the seeds, carry them off,
and feed on the protein, in the process planting the cacti in
new locations.

Research by a colleague of ours at Colorado State University, Joan Herbers, indicates that any given ant is quite unlikely to perform all of these tasks. In fact each ant is, to a degree, a specialist. The largest workers are the builders and foragers for prey and carrion. Most of the harvesting of honeydew on plants is done by slightly smaller workers with slightly less orange-brown coloration. The still smaller, all-black workers one sometimes sees on the nest evidently are nurses that spend most of their time inside the nest. The three kinds of workers are called "majors," "medias," and "minors," in the usual jargon of myrmecologists. The three castes are by no means sharply differentiated in color or size, but they do tend to specialize in behavior. Indeed, individual ants tend to perform the same duty and in the same place consistently. Joan Herbers marked over a thousand ants from the same nest, using different colored paint marks according to the trees on which they foraged for honeydew. Over several days, a high percentage of the ants returned to the same trees; only 7 percent were found performing other tasks in other places.

Students of ants often have to paint-mark a great many ants in order to find out exactly what is going on. Kevin O'Neill, of Montana State University, marked thirteen hundred ants from five nests in the same area, hoping to discover to what extent ants from nearby nests represented one colony or several. He found that there was much interchange of workers among these nests, with no conspicuous aggression, indicating that one colony of closely related individuals may occupy several nests. But when workers from a different group of nests are introduced, much fighting occurs.

So prevalent are ants—the most abundant form of life on earth—and their lives so complex and mediated mostly by chemical cues we can detect only by refined techniques—that their study is usually left to myrmecologists. Only now and then, and with great patience, may non-specialists dip into their lives a bit. Our neighbors may have considered us strange that we spent so much time gazing at ant hills, but they lacked our respect for these remarkable creatures. In the ant, evolution has produced the ultimate organism, far less concerned with self-examination than we are and doubtless well able to flourish long after we have said adieu to a planet we never learned to occupy without destroying.

3

Hummingbirds

THE ARRIVAL OF THE FIRST hummingbird was always an event, never predictable with accuracy. Over the years the first one appeared as early as April 18 and as late as May 6. On at least three occasions there were substantial snowstorms after he had appeared, and in 1990 the temperature dropped to 17 degrees a few days after he had arrived. That these delicate birds survive under these conditions is something to marvel at, especially as there are few flowers yet in bloom—a few pasque flowers, sand lilies, and spring beauties, and not much else. Of course we put out our feeder as soon as they arrived, or a bit before, using a cup of sugar to a pint of water, plus a little red coloring. One year, when we had been away up to the first of May, a hummer was already circling the hook on which we usually hung our feeder. Evidently he had remembered where he had found sugar water the year before. The early arrivals were always male broad-tailed hummingbirds. The females arrived a week or two later.

When the first hummers arrived we could count on hearing our first mourning doves and house wrens, perhaps also a rock wren holding forth from a granite outcrop and a green-tailed towhee from a bushy hillside. So there was much to celebrate. No doubt there would be cold days ahead (in 1991 there was a little snow on June 9!) but once started, spring would not turn back.

Like all hummingbirds, broad-tails are feisty and the males actively defend the territories they have selected. In flight, the males produce a whistle as the air rushes through a slot between their outer two major wing feathers, which are slender and tapered. It has been assumed that the wing-sounds play a major role in territory defense. Two researchers, Sarah Miller and David Inouye, working at the Rocky Mountain Biological Station, near Crested Butte, Colorado, set about to elucidate the function of the wing-sounds. Selected males were silenced by closing off the slits in the wings with a thin film of glue. The glue did not deter flight and could easily be removed with acetone. Silenced males were less aggressive than normal males and often lost their territories, apparently because they could not communicate threat and because their normal behavior was disturbed by their awareness that they were silent. When their whistle was restored, they returned to normal territorial defense.

Males defend their territories by circuit flights about the area and by making "pendulum dives," in which they rise many feet in the air and plunge downward at great speed, pulling out of their dive only when they seem precariously close to the ground or to bushes. Despite their small size, hummingbirds are evidently well endowed with sex hormones. Both males and females also produce a chirping sound when feeding or when pursuing one another. To persons fortunate to be living or hiking in the Rockies, there are no more welcome sounds than those of hummingbirds.

Hummingbirds were one of the more amazing discoveries of the first Europeans to visit the Americas. They had seen nothing like them, birds so tiny, so brilliantly colored, so electric in their energy, so various in their forms. In Europe they became favorite ornaments in ladies' hats, and in high circles it was fashionable to have a cabinet of stuffed hummingbirds. In one year, a London merchant imported four hundred thousand skins from the New World. After 1861, John Gould's volume of vividly colored humming-birds became a fixture in Victorian parlors. Fortunately tastes have changed.

Discovery of the broad-tailed hummingbird is credited to Meriwether Lewis, who found a nest with eggs as he was returning through Idaho with other members of the Corps of Discovery in June 1806. The broad-tail is a bird of western mountains, spending winters in Central America. No doubt they nested near our house every summer, but the only nest we found was on the low branch of a pine some distance away. Nests are so small and so neatly camouflaged that discovering one requires a good deal of luck.

In his book *The Life of the Hummingbird*, Alexander Skutch tells us that broad-tails weigh in at about 4.3 grams, a bit more than the ruby-throats of the East and the rufous hummingbirds that visited our feeders in July and August. The largest is the giant hummingbird of the Andes (20 grams and 8 inches in length), the smallest the bee hummingbird of Cuba (2 grams and 2.5 inches long). By far the majority of species live in Central and South America, but not necessarily in tropical forests; some occur up to fifteen thousand feet in the Andes. We well remember watching hummingbirds at a feeder in a Costa Rican cloud forest. In an hour or two we recorded the green hermit, the violet sabrewing, the purple-throated mountain gem, the green-crowned brilliant, and the magenta-throated woodstar. The extravagant names suggest their extravagant plumage, but do nothing to describe their bills, which vary from relatively short to half as long as the body, straight or curved like a sickle. We have seen, at home and in the tropics, only a tiny fraction of the three hundred twenty known species of hummingbirds. Seventeen species breed in the United States.

At his farm in southern Costa Rica, Alexander Skutch found seventeen species resident or casual, and got to know some of them very well. Some of them formed singing assemblies, each male perched on a separate branch of a tree and chirping for hours at a time, trying to attract a female to his perch. In the tropics there are many "hummingbird flowers," the blossoms of which are pollinated by hummers especially adapted to visit them with respect to bill length and curvature. Typical hummingbird flowers are tubular, scentless, and often red in color, in contrast to bee flowers with their open corollas, powerful scents, and often white or yellow colors.

Generally it is the male that displays brilliant colors, as it would not do if the female did not blend with the nest while incubating the eggs. Males of many species (including the broad-tail) have dark throat patches that in certain lights reflect shades of blue, purple, or scarlet. These are structural colors similar to the blues of butterflies, produced by light reflected from delicate striations on the feathers or scales. Browns and grays, and the dark backing of structural colors, are pigmental.

Active hummingbirds require a steady diet of carbohydrates to fuel their bodies. They are said to have the greatest output of energy, gram for gram, of any animal, and to burn calories fifty times more rapidly than the average human. So a hummingbird, whether courting, defending a territory, feeding its young, or just surviving, must visit nectar-bearing flowers, or a feeder, many times during the day. Fortunately some of the fuel can be stored as fat, enabling the bird to survive short lean periods or to undertake long flights. Resting hummingbirds, of course, require fewer calories.

The secret of the their ability to survive the variable climate of North America, or of mountainous terrain, lies in their capacity to become torpid. A hummingbird's usual body temperature is 102–108 degrees Fahrenheit, but a sleeping bird, at night or on a cool, cloudy day, may undergo a drop in temperature of several degrees, even at times close to air temperature. They are able to recover in a short time from a hypothermia that would be fatal to humans and most other mammals. A torpid bird cannot fly, but must warm up to at least 86 degrees to be able to do so. Presumably they are able to shiver their flight muscles to produce body heat, as bumblebees do.

Few birds are able to undergo a loss of body heat to anywhere near this extent. One bird that can is the poorwill, a relative of the nighthawks and whippoorwills, that we heard calling occasionally when we slept on our deck. Torpid poorwills have been found during the colder months of the year, their body temperature reduced to half the normal. It is interesting that students of bird evolution have concluded that hummingbirds and poorwills, as different as they are in behavior and appearance, may have shared a remote common ancestry.

It is not often appreciated that hummingbirds eat a great many insects. These form an especially important part of the diet when young are being fed, as growth requires protein. In our study of dance flies, discussed in another chapter, we often saw hummers entering the swarm and picking off flies one by one. Insects are also plucked from vegetation, or sucked up with the nectar from flowers. One researcher kept a captive hummingbird and fed it only sugar water, but it declined in health. When fruit flies were put in the cage, they were devoured eagerly, and the hummer's health improved dramatically. Hummingbirds are believed also to profit from enzymes and vitamins in the nectar of flowers. Surprisingly, these tiny birds may live as long as ten years if they are able to overcome the many hazards facing them: storms, predators, or being caught in spider webs or on sticky plants.

It doesn't take more than a few minutes of observation to note that hummingbirds can fly backwards as well as forwards, that they can fly straight up and down, can change direction abruptly, and can hover. However, they can't walk or hop, nor can they soar on their slender wings. Their wings beat twenty to eighty times a second, and allow them to fly up to thirty miles an hour, perhaps twice that much during a dive.

Although broad-tails are the only kind that breed in our area, in midsummer they are joined by a migrant, the rufous hummingbird. These reddish-golden sprites breed in the Far West, from northern California well into coastal Alaska. In the spring they migrate up the coast from Mexico, but by mid-July the males begin to move south again, this time through the Rockies. Though smaller than the broad-tails, these males are fiercely aggressive and tend to drive the broad-tails from feeders. We often watched a male perched on the top of a nearby tree, ready to dash after any hummingbird that usurped "his" feeder. Some people call these hummers "the red menace," and have been known to use a garden hose to discourage them. We accepted and enjoyed them, though we sometimes wondered if the broad-tails were getting enough juice to sustain themselves. No doubt they did, as they stayed with us until early September, some weeks after the last rufous had left.

In terms of body length, rufous hummingbirds have the longest migrations of any bird. According to Bill Calder, of the University of Arizona, who has been studying these birds for years, they may fly about forty-nine million body-lengths during their migrations. Working at the Rocky Mountain Biological Station, near Crested Butte, Colorado, he has found that banded individuals sometimes return to the very same patch of wildflowers they visited the previous summer—a remarkable memory for a reliable food source.

In August they begin to accumulate fat preparatory to their migration to Mexico. The birds add to their weight by two-thirds, says Calder, "but that increment is only two grams of fat." Once fattened, the bird may fly five hundred miles without refueling, in still air. Like many birds, hummers often time their flights to take advantage of tail winds.

Both broad-tailed and rufous hummingbirds depend upon wildflowers (or feeders) for their sustenance, and during migratory flights they must refuel periodically. Now that so many roads and trails penetrate the Rockies, and so many homes are built in places that were once pristine, we wonder what the future of our hummingbirds may be.

4

Caterpillar-hunters

"IN NO WAY CAN the tents of tent caterpillars be viewed as beautiful," writes Vincent Dethier in his fine little book, *The World of the Tent Makers.* "They are exquisitely constructed of finest gossamer, marvelously engineered, cunningly adapted to need, but monuments to ugliness." By the end of June, when the caterpillars have left, the silk is gray and tattered, the tents filled with fecal pellets and cast skins, and the bushes on which they fed are largely denuded of leaves. The caterpillars themselves are by no means things of beauty, sparsely covered as they are with long hairs, but close examination reveals a pattern of subtle colors that can be appreciated if one can forgive the undesirable activities of the caterpillars.

Dethier's book discusses the eastern tent caterpillar, which is most fond of cherries and other fruit trees, though more than fifty kinds of trees and bushes are known to be attacked. Our western tent caterpillars resemble their eastern cousins in most respects, but locally they are most abundant on squaw currants, bitterbrush, and chokecherries. Since we used to harvest the currants and chokecherries each year for making jelly, we did not appreciate the inroads the caterpillars made on our winter breakfast menu. A single tent-full of caterpillars can denude the better part of a bush. Most of our hillsides were covered with currants and bitterbrush, and during some years they were uglified with the tents of caterpillars.

Like many insects, tent caterpillars have years of abundance and years of relative scarcity. Perhaps severe winters or unseasonable ice storms kill off some of the egg clusters on the bushes or the small caterpillars when they emerge. Tent caterpillars are susceptible to viruses and bacterial diseases, the enemies of any creatures that live in crowded conditions. Several tiny wasps are known to attack the eggs, and several other wasps and tachina flies attack the larvae. When the caterpillars are abundant, the parasites thrive and produce more of their kind, so that there are fewer caterpillars the next year.

When the caterpillars approach full size, they leave their tents and the silken threads leading from them. Then they crawl about freely, nibbling at diverse plants and eventually seeking a place to spin their cocoons. It is at this time that a much larger wasp makes its appearance and begins to attack them. *Podalonia occidentalis* (which might be roughly translated "western long-legs") is about three-quarters of an inch long, black and red, with a slender "waist" like that of many wasps. So far as is known, the species is a specialist on western tent caterpillars. There are reports from New Mexico, Colorado, Alberta, Nevada, and California, all indicating an association with tent caterpillars and no other species. Since the wasps must be active at exactly the right time, the two to three week period when the caterpillars are full-size and out of their tents, their development must be timed quite precisely. Locally these wasps appear each year in mid-June and are gone by the fourth of July. We were always on the alert for them and have never seen them at any other time. How their life cycle and that of the caterpillars are so well-synchronized we have no idea.

Male podalonias are a bit more slender than the females. We sometimes saw them patrolling hillsides where there were tent caterpillars. Now and then a male would descend upon a female, riding astride her and holding her around the neck with his mandibles while trying to make genital contact. An observer in Nevada, where there was a large outbreak of tent caterpillars, noted about forty males in a struggling ball around a hapless female. We often saw both males and females taking nectar from the flowers of miners' candles (*Cryptantha*), which are in bloom during the active period of the wasps.

Females spend much of their time searching about on and near bushes where tent caterpillars have been active. When a caterpillar is sighted, the wasp leaps upon it and stings it several times, starting near one end and proceeding toward the other. The caterpillar is soon flaccid, and the wasp picks it up with her mandibles and straddles it, holding it slightly off the ground with her stout legs. Since the caterpillar is longer than the wasp, it protrudes both in front and behind, and the pair make a startling appearance as they proceed over the ground. Within a few minutes the wasp drops the caterpillar, either on the ground or more often in a clump of grass or in the crotch of a plant. She then searches about for a place to dig a nest. She digs a little here and there, testing the soil for its friability, and may revisit her prey once or twice while she is doing this. With vigorous thrusts of her front legs, which bear rake-like spines, she scrapes the soil away; when stones are encountered they are lifted out with her mandibles. Once a hole is started, it takes only ten minutes or so to complete, and the caterpillar is picked up and carried to the edge of the hole. Then the wasp enters and pulls the prey in head first. A few minutes later she emerges and begins to fill the hole by scraping in soil from the edge of the burrow. This only takes three to five minutes, and the wasp then cleans herself and flies off.

We marked several nests and dug them out, reluctantly since we appreciated what the wasps were doing, but curious to study their contents. Within each burrow, only two or three inches deep, we found a small cell in which the caterpillar had been placed in a coiled position. The wasp's egg, laid on the side of the prey, hatched in about two days, and the larva, pale and grub-like, consumed the caterpillar in about ten days. Then it spun a cocoon in which it remained for nearly a year, emerging as a wasp only when something triggered its emergence to coincide with tent caterpillars that have just left their webs.

Sometimes the wasps seemed unable to find prey right away, especially when most of the caterpillars had spun their cocoons. In this case they often dug their nest first and filled it some time later, or left it abandoned. This versatility (prey first or nest first) is unusual for a digger wasp: most wasp species seem locked in one or the other sequence of behavior.

Podalonia occidentalis has only two or three weeks in which to hunt its caterpillars, so females must be active every day, filling a nest or two. But their efforts are thwarted by their own enemies. One summer we dug out twelve nests and found nine of them infested with the maggots of small parasitic flies. These flies perch nearby when the wasp is working at the nest, then dash in quickly and deposit minute maggots on the prey. In the nest, the maggots grow rapidly and destroy the wasp's egg as well as the caterpillar. It seems odd that so efficient a predator should sacrifice so many of its eggs and prey to these flies. Their bravado, attacking a caterpillar as large as themselves, is subverted by the stealth of tiny flies, and the wasps act as if they were unaware of their presence.

Occidentalis is only one of several species of its genus that occurs in our area. *Podalonia luctuosa* is in fact one of our harbingers of spring, appearing as it does on warm days in March and April, when further snows are likely. (The word *luctuosa* is Latin for "mournful," presumably reflecting the jet-black coloration of these wasps; but we rejoiced on seeing them so early in the spring—our first wasps.) Females have spent the winter in deep burrows in the soil and are out early to hunt for cutworm caterpillars before they spin their cocoons to produce the moths of summer. Cutworms are naked, rather greasy and unattractive caterpillars that live in the soil and come out at night to nip off small, growing plants. *Luctuosa* is one of only a very few wasps that overwinter as an adult; almost all others spend the winter in cocoons and emerge when spring and summer days are warmer.

Since we had no garden, we could watch the wasps and hope for a good supply of cutworms. But farmers and gardeners do not appreciate having their young plants nipped off during the night. Years ago (1930) a federal entomologist, E.J. Newcomer, studied the wasps in his garden near Yakima, Washington. He described their behavior well.

"*Luctuosa* hunts rapidly, almost feverishly, running from grass clump to grass clump, inspecting the ground carefully, for the cutworms she seeks are nocturnal feeders, and lie hidden by day. She knows when she has found a cutworm's hiding place, and she digs frantically, using her fore legs, and throwing the dirt back like a dog digging for a squirrel. She soon uncovers the luckless worm and drags it forth, twisting and squirming."

We often witnessed this small drama along our roads and hillsides, but we are uncertain as to how the wasps detect the cutworms. Since the wasp's antennae are in constant motion, we suspect that she detects the odor of the cutworm through an inch or two of soil. When the prey is exhumed, it is stung several times along the underside of the body. Since the

walking legs, the true legs of the thorax and the fleshy "pro-
legs" of the abdomen, are strung out along the underside, the
stings are actually applied in such a way that the legs are
soon immobilized. Also, the cutworm's nerve ganglia are
similarly strung out along the underside of the body. In any
case the cutworm soon becomes flaccid and is picked up and
carried to a place of concealment while the wasp digs a shal-
low nest very much like that of *occidentalis*. By nesting early
in the spring, *luctuosa* may avoid some of the fly parasites
that haunt other members of the genus.

Another species of *Podalonia* occurred around our home
occasionally. This was *valida* (a Latin word meaning
"strong," reflecting the larger size and more formidable
demeanor of this species). *Valida* is a specialist on large,
densely hairy caterpillars, more specifically the yellow
woollybear, also called the saltmarsh caterpillar. Salt marshes
are not prevalent in Colorado, but these caterpillars can be
found almost everywhere, feeding in midsummer on a great
variety of herbaceous plants, including many crop plants. In
late summer the caterpillars spin cocoons that produce
attractive yellowish moths speckled with dark spots. As in
the case of tent caterpillars, there are far fewer moths than
caterpillars, as many fall to predators, parasites, and disease.

Neither salt marsh caterpillars nor their predator,
Podalonia valida, were seen often around our mountain
home, but during some years both are abundant on the
plains not far to the east. We remember one summer on the
Pawnee Grasslands when the caterpillars were defoliating
the sweet clover everywhere. It was easy to spot podalonias
grappling with their large, hairy prey, then carrying them
off to their nesting sites. Since salt marsh caterpillars are
about two inches long, and *valida* nearly as large, the pair
made an impressive sight as they trundled over the ground.
It appeared that each female wasp selected a bare spot on

the prairie as her nesting area and over a few days made a series of nests, perhaps a dozen or more, within a few inches of one another. Prey was taken only after a nest had been made ready to contain it, a reversal of the usual behavior in most species of *Podalonia*. The nesting sites were defended vigorously from invaders such as other *valida* females, ants, or peregrinating beetles. The defensive postures of the wasps were striking: they stood on "tip toes" with their abdomen elevated and their wings extended, all the while facing the intruder and even grappling with it if it did not retreat. Active defense of a nesting site is rare among solitary wasps, but common among social wasps such as yellow jackets. Unfortunately, like other podalonias, *valida* is not highly responsive to the fly parasites that haunt the nesting site, and a considerable percentage of offspring may succumb to the attacks of maggots.

To a student of insects, it is satisfying to find that related species of wasps, defined only by color and minor structural differences, differ in major aspects of behavior. One takes naked, subterranean cutworms, another takes sparsely hairy tent-makers, while a third takes free-living woollybears. Of the three, *valida* is unique in preparing a series of nests in a plot that is defended against intruders, and in preparing a nest before taking prey. Each has an emergence time closely tuned to that of its prey. Knowledge of no species is complete until one knows what it does for a living and how it interacts with other species and responds to its physical environment. That is why entomologists, amateur or professional, are devoted to distraction by their subjects of study; they know how much they still have to learn, and what pleasure there is in the learning.

5

Owls

PERSONAL ENCOUNTERS with owls are far too rare. These are the most mysterious of birds—and the most beneficial, since they feed mostly on rodents. Presumably the legend of the "wise old owl" arose from their stoic posture and their large eyes, spaced on a broad face to provide binocular vision. That owls are feared by small mammals and birds is suggested by the fact that some moths and even caterpillars have "eye spots" of contrasting colors that they display suddenly when disturbed—"playing owl." Experiments have shown that small birds do, in fact, avoid potential prey when eye spots are painted on them.

Our most intimate contact with owls occurred one early summer day when we were eating our lunch at a favorite spot beneath a leaning Douglas-fir. Halfway through our sandwiches we glanced up to discover four young saw-whet owls, each perched on a different branch and all seeming to stare at us. Each was handsomely garbed in rich brown, with a white breast and a pair of white eyebrows. They seemed full-sized (not very large for a saw-whet) and probably could fly perfectly well, but they evidently did not consider us a threat. The next morning they were gone.

It seemed probable that they had come from a nest nearby, and since there was an old, mostly dead pine not far away that had a big hole in it about thirty feet up, we wondered if that might have been their home. Fortunately we knew an owl enthusiast, David Palmer, so we asked him if he would like to investigate our supposed owl nest (especially since we had no desire to climb the tree, and he was forty years younger). Indeed he found that the hole was filled with pellets, the skin and bones of the rodents they had consumed.

We never saw that brood of saw-whets again, nor did they ever nest nearby again so far as we know. But we sometimes heard their long-repeated "too too too" from distant hillsides. One night we heard their rasping calls (supposed to sound like a saw being whetted) outside our bedroom window. We went out and tried to locate the owls and did pursue them from tree to tree, though it was dark enough that they seemed no more than balls of fluff.

Another close contact occurred one day as we sat at our desks doing something or other and heard a disturbance in a small pine outside our windows. Chickadees and nuthatches were hopping about the tree with a great deal of chattering, and among the branches stood a pygmy owl, hardly larger than a couple of adjacent pine cones. He was doing nothing to threaten the birds, but mobbing of owls is a common behavior of birds. On another occasion, on a hike up a favorite canyon, we saw a pygmy owl carrying a recent kill, once again surrounded by chattering small birds.

Several hypotheses have been proposed to explain why birds so frequently mob owls. Perhaps most likely is the "move on" hypothesis. Some owls do attack and eat birds, and it is to the advantage of birds to persuade owls to go elsewhere. A single bird could hardly have much influence on an owl, but a group of birds, noisily flitting from one branch to another, could well be persuasive; in fact the owls often do move on. There is little evidence that owls attack swarming birds, but if they remain in the area they may well pick off a sleeping bird.

Pygmy owls are not only improbably small but they defy the definition of owl by being mostly diurnal. Like the saw-whets, they sing in early summer with a series of soft hoots, which we often heard from nearby woods. The vocal repertory of these small owls is not at all like the hoots of the great horned owl, which we often heard at night. In late winter pairs of great-horns would "sing" to one another, each on a slightly different pitch. There is something spooky about owl calls, but none of our local owls can rival the barred owls we have sometimes heard on camping trips in states farther east.

One who became especially intimate with an owl is Bernd Heinrich, a versatile naturalist whom we will meet again in the chapter on bumblebees. Bernd Heinrich found a small great horned owl that had fallen from its nest following a storm. He adopted it, naming it "bubo" (the generic name of these owls) and feeding it primarily on road kills. Most of the time it lived in a cardboard box in Heinrich's cabin, and when Heinrich changed camp, the owl went along in his box on the back seat of a jeep. After a few weeks he was allowed limited and finally full freedom, though he stayed close to the cabin for some time. The bond of affection that developed lasted through three summers. By that time the owl was more than able to feed himself, and he left for the last time. Heinrich tells of this with delightful prose and excellent sketches and photographs in his book *One Man's Owl*. Others have found that owls make good pets, but it is illegal to take birds from the wild as pets (unless one has a permit to conduct research, as Heinrich did).

The great horned owl and several other species have "horns" or "ears," consisting of paired tufts of feathers on top of the head. These can be raised and lowered, and probably play a role in communication to other owls and to potential enemies. When a "horned" owl is disturbed, the tufts are elevated. Perhaps they also play a role in courtship and in enhancing the cryptic form and color of the owls which, when at rest, look rather like stumps or clumps of leaves.

Owls often hunt along roads, since small rodents that cross the road are easily spotted. Owls do see reasonably well at night, but they also rely heavily on hearing. The large ears on the sides of the face are spaced to provide binaural hearing, and owls often swivel their heads to scan for the sounds of rodents scurrying in the leaf litter. Working with barn owls, Roger Payne showed that in total darkness owls are still effective predators. But when he plugged their ears, the owls went wide of their mark. Roger Payne went on to become well known for his study of communication in hump-backed whales. We knew him long ago, in the "owl" phase of his career.

Now and then, while studying insects in the Pawnee National Grasslands, we looked up to see a burrowing owl perched on a fencepost, rather unowlish with his long legs. Members of the Long Expedition of 1820 often saw these owls near colonies of prairie dogs and speculated that they might prey on the "dogs." Eventually they shot one and studied its stomach, finding it full of grasshopper wings and pieces of other insects. They rightly concluded that the owls often live near prairie dogs in order to make use of abandoned burrows. Now that prairie dogs have been eliminated from most of their former habitat (sometimes simply for "sport"), burrowing owls are becoming an increasingly rare sight.

The great gray owl and the snowy owl are large owls of the Far North, both lacking the "horns" of the great horned owl and several other species. On cold winter days these owls sometimes stray into our northern states, and we well remember the excitement of seeing a snowy owl now and then when we lived in the Northeast. In the tropics there are owls of many kinds, including several that specialize in catching fish, in somewhat the manner of a fishing eagle.

Nowadays the most publicized owl is the northern spotted owl of the Pacific Northwest. These are large owls of mature old-growth forests, where they nest in the broken-off tops of fallen trees and live mostly on red-backed voles. In 1979 a group of scientists, working to implement the National Forest Management Act, selected the northern spotted owl as an "indicator species," that is, a species especially characteristic of an ecosystem (with all the many other species unique to the system). In this case the ecosystem also included the marbled murrelet, a sea bird that idiosyncratically nests in these same forests. In 1987 environmental groups asked the Fish and Wildlife Service to list the owl as threatened, under the Endangered Species Act. When the FWS declined, the matter was taken to court. The unsuspecting owl became the plaintiff in Federal District Court in Seattle, in *Northern Spotted Owl v Hodel*. Although the owl won the case, the FWS failed to designate critical habitat, and "owl" took the case to court again in *Northern Spotted Owl v Lujan*. Now that the owl had had all that experience in court, the FWS was persuaded to designate 11.6 million acres of forest to ensure survival of the owl.

The acreage was later considerably reduced, but in spite of this many loggers found themselves out of jobs. Labeling the whole procedure a "gimmick" dreamed up by environmentalists, they took to the streets, to the press, and to their congressmen. The poor spotted owl was demonized, when in fact most old-growth forest had already been cut and, without protection, the rest would be gone in a decade or two. The lumber industry was already depending heavily on fast-growing pines from plantations in the southeastern states. In his fine book *Crossing the Next Meridian*, Charles Wilkinson quotes a former manager of Weyerhaeuser Corporation:

"Weyerhaeuser made a fortune from old growth, but you can't cut the last one and say, 'Gee, that was nice. What do we do now?'"

The spotted owl is one of more than twenty species of owls, throughout the world, that are threatened or close to extinction. In every case loss of habitat is cited as reason for their decline. Owls must have space in which to hunt, and habitat containing an abundance of prey. Owls are very special birds, an apogee of evolution that must be treasured. To camp in the wild and not hear an owl, or to tell our children that the owls of legend and folklore are gone like the dinosaurs, would be a tragedy indeed.

6

Bumblebees

SPRING BRINGS THE bumblebees from their wintering sites, searching about for a cavity in which to start a nest. These are queens that mated the previous summer. In a few weeks they and their smaller daughters (workers) will fill the meadows, collecting great globs of pollen on their hind legs. We found eight common species in our meadows, four of them black and yellow, four of them black, yellow, and orange. These are both "warning patterns," serving as signals that these are insects with potent stings. Black and yellow banding occurs in yellow jacket wasps, some caterpillars, and other disagreeable insects, while orange occurs in monarch butterflies, box elder bugs, and other distasteful insects. Having developed the basic black and yellow pattern, some kinds of bumblebees went a step further and added orange, as if to stress their message. That birds and toads do learn to avoid warningly colored insects has been well established by experiments. People, too, have learned to avoid close contact with bumblebees, though unless they are actually handled, bumblebees will go about their business with little regard for us.

What would a meadow of wildflowers be without the drone of bumblebees? Indeed, many of our wildflowers would be hard put to survive without bumblebees to pollinate them. Flowers with deep blossoms, such as penstemons and pink bergamot, require pollinators with long tongues able to reach deep within them. In one study of pollinator ecology, it was shown that if clovers, lupines, and paintbrushes are caged to prevent the entry of bumblebees, they set little or no fruit.

Bumblebees seem the epitome of nature at its most beautiful and efficient. The very name bumblebee (as well as its Latin equivalent, *Bombus*) seems eminently fitting for these bumbling bombs of energy. As if aware that summer is all too short, the queens set about promptly to establish a nest, often in an abandoned rodent nest. Using their ability to produce wax from glands between the abdominal segments, they prepare a cell in which pollen is placed and several eggs laid. When the eggs hatch, the larvae are fed honey from waxen pots the queen has also prepared. As the larvae grow, the cell becomes swollen, and soon they spin cocoons there. The bees that emerge are smaller than the queen and will serve as workers, taking over much of the collection of nectar and pollen as well as many of the nest duties.

The workers vary a good deal in size, and the larger ones often have well-developed ovaries and the capacity to lay eggs. The queen prevents this and asserts her dominance by head-butting, biting, and grappling. The larger workers do most of the foraging, while the smaller ones serve as nurses, at least for the first few days. If the queen dies, or is removed by an experimenter, the larger workers will lay eggs. Since they haven't mated, they will produce males, since in Hymenoptera unfertilized eggs produce only males (with a few exceptions). By midsummer, the queen herself will have laid some unfertilized, male-producing eggs, and larger, potential queen females will be produced, the foundation of next summer's brood of bumblebees.

So the nest is a busy place, and the goings-on are by no means identical in different species of bumblebees. It is not easy to study the nests; not only is there danger of being stung but one invariably disturbs the bee family badly by opening the nest. Various researchers have induced bumblebees to nest in boxes not unlike bird houses. These can be designed so that they can be opened easily and the nest contents studied through the season. Also, if one places such boxes around fields of red clover or other crops, he can improve pollination. Boxes must be supplied with chopped-up straw, or the contents of rodent nests, as the queen depends upon this material to surround her cells and brood. Nest boxes are placed just below the ground surface, with an entranceway provided, or under logs or bushes. Two researchers, R.E. Fye and J.T. Medler, put out 154 artificial nests of various designs in Wisconsin and had about a third of them occupied by bumblebees.

One year I decided to try my hand at inducing bumblebees to nest in boxes. Not being much of a carpenter, I made only six, which I put out early in spring along the edge of a meadow that was frequented by bumblebees each summer. I had hoped for at least one-third acceptance, but evidently I failed to meet the bumblebees' requirements, as none were occupied. I did make the acquaintance of a particularly fine prairie rattlesnake that lived beneath a rocky outcrop where I had placed a nest box.

One of the more admirable features of bumblebees is their ability to fly when temperatures are decidedly cool, even close to freezing. On our hikes into Colorado's high country, we have seen bumblebees on the wing well above timberline, where they visit the flowers of alpine clover, sky pilot, and other diminutive plants. One of the species occurring there ranges north to beyond the arctic circle.

There are a few tropical bumblebees, but most inhabit cool climes, where the summer season is short and the weather unpredictable. Here they need not wait for warm, sunny days, as they must be on the wing as often as possible. Yet they cannot fly when their flight muscles are much below 85 degrees Fahrenheit. They are not only able to maintain such a flight temperature, but a resting bee, whose temperature is close to that of the air, is able to acquire the necessary warmth and take flight within a short time. This is accomplished by "shivering," that is, by rapid contractions of the flight muscles. These are temporarily dissociated from the wings, so that the wings do not move, and the only indication of warm-up is a pumping of the abdomen, which serves to increase the flow of oxygen.

During flight, heat loss is prevented, in part, by the dense hairs on the body. Also, the bees are able to close off a valve that reduces the blood flowing to the abdomen, helping to keep the heat in the flight muscles of the thorax. To prevent overheating, the valve can be opened, permitting the flow of blood into the abdomen, where the hairs are thinner and the blood cooled. The "heat exchanger" also serves a valuable function in the nest, as bumblebees are able to curl their bodies over their brood and convey heat to them—a rare example of an insect that actually incubates its nestlings. Still more rarely, recently emerged males of at least one species may assist in warming the brood in a similar manner. Parental care of any kind is rare among insects.

To Bernd Heinrich, a professor at the University of Vermont, belongs the credit for elucidating the ways in which bumblebees thrive in cool environments and take the best advantage of their resources. In his fascinating book *The Thermal Warriors*, he tells of the large wooly bumblebee *Bombus solaris*, which occurs on Ellesmere Island, far north of the Arctic Circle, where the daytime temperatures rarely exceed 40 degrees Fahrenheit. Here the queen must survive a very long winter and rear a new brood in no more than six weeks of summer. Using body heat produced by shivering and abdomen-pumping, she provides the larvae with a near-tropical environment in which to grow, and may even accelerate the growth of the eggs in her ovaries before the birth of the larvae.

Bumblebees have no recruitment system similar to that of honey bees. Each bee explores the environment and moves from one flower to another, stopping where there are rewards in terms of pollen and nectar. Worker bees vary a good deal in size, as I have said, and queens are larger still. Tongue lengths vary with body size, and individuals with longer tongues are able to exploit the flowers with the deepest blossoms. Individuals learn which blossoms are productive and which have nectaries that can be reached readily. So they tend to revisit flowers of the same kind and are therefore effective pollinators. Bumblebee colonies are active for only a few short months and rarely have more than a dozen or two workers, so they must work hard to supply food for the growing larvae, their investment in a new generation of males and potential queens. Despite their name, bumblebees cannot afford to bumble!

Beginning in midsummer, males make their appearance and begin to fill their role in mating with virgin females that will become the queens of next spring. Males of several species fly along established routes, pausing here and there, on trees and bushes, to deposit a scent from glands in their heads. This behavior was noted long ago by Charles Darwin, who found that they continued to visit these sites even though he had altered the appearance of the sites. Most scent-marking occurs first thing in the morning and is repeated each day. The same flight route may be used from year to year, and even the same object may be marked year by year, even though these are bees of subsequent generations. Virgin females visit these sites and are intercepted by males, who mate with them. The sexually attractive scents have been identified for more than a dozen species of bumblebees. In every case they consist of a mixture of complex, volatile, organic compounds. Mating between members of different species is prevented by chemical differences in the scents, by differences in flight paths, and by differences in the height of the deposits above the ground.

Several years ago I discovered that several of our common local species of bumblebees behave quite differently. I found males perching on the tops of bushes and tall weeds in nearby meadows. From time to time they flew off, especially in response to passing insects (or even birds)—or to stones that I tossed near them. In these species, males have especially large eyes, which serve them well in spotting intruders in their territories. With the help of two colleagues, I set about to figure out exactly what was going on.

We found that as soon as the sun hits the meadow in the morning, males select a perch and begin to move up and down along stems and leaves of plants surrounding their perch, covering an area of one or two yards. We marked each territory with a numbered stake and marked each male with a spot of colored paint on the back of his thorax. Some males were collected in solvent so that we could find the source of the scent they were applying to vegetation and, hopefully, identify the chemistry of the scent. We also collected samples of the vegetation and analyzed their chemistry, hoping to demonstrate that the scent was, in fact, being deposited there.

Each male returned to the same perch each morning, for a week or more. Each morning he scent-marked nearby plants vigorously for an hour or two, less frequently later in the morning. Between and following scent-marking, males assumed an "alert" posture on their perch, their wings extended slightly, their antennae extended rigidly forward, and their body tilted upward slightly. They often rotated on their perch, presumably to scan their territory for intruders, who were sometimes pursued several yards from the perch. Males in adjacent territories often attacked one another, sometimes rising several feet in the air as they engaged in aerial combat. Now and then a male succeeded in usurping a territory from another male. If a female passed over the territory, she was quickly seized and forced to the ground, where a noisy mating took place.

The three species we studied all had very similar behavior, and the territories were sometimes intermingled. The scents proved to be generally similar to those produced by bumblebee species that mark routes, but each species had its own medley of chemical components. We were especially intrigued by this because we had observed very similar scent-marking and territorial defense in a genus of wasps, the beewolves. Territorial scent-marking is, in the broad view, rather an unusual strategy for bringing the sexes together. Evidently members of two quite unrelated groups have evolved this behavior independently.

There is no better way to spend a summer day than browsing in a meadow rich with diverse vegetation accompanied by the hum of insects. Bees and butterflies of many kinds are visiting wildflowers; dragonflies and robber flies are hawking prey; and male bumblebees are luring females with their subtle fragrances. It is, as always, much more meaningful when one knows the plants and the insects, not only their names but their ways of life. Each is playing a role unique to itself, yet impinging on other residents of the meadow in diverse ways. There are endless stories waiting to be told, scripts to be deciphered.

The meadow in which we studied bumblebees has now become part of a housing development—a by no means unexpected occurrence in a society quite ready to trash the environment whenever convenient.

But bumblebees have not always been held in such low regard. In *The Origin of Species*, Charles Darwin remarked that bumblebees are largely responsible for the pollination of red clover. But their nests are often destroyed by field mice, and since cats destroy mice, bumblebees tend to be most numerous near villages. Darwin's "bulldog," Thomas Henry Huxley, facetiously suggested that since spinsters keep cats, it follows that the more spinsters, the more red clover. Meanwhile, Darwin's German supporter Ernst Haeckel quipped that British power depended upon bumblebees, because they pollinated the red clover on which cattle feed, and the navy subsists largely on beef!

To poets, there is magic in bumblebees. To Emerson, the bumblebee was a paragon of good living.

> Burly, dosing bumble-bee,
> Where thou art is clime for me.
> Let them sail for Porto Rique,
> Far-off heats through seas to seek;
> I will follow thee alone,
> Thou animated torrid zone! ...

Today, who speaks for the bumblebee?

7

Wrens

HOUSE WRENS SEEM unable to contain themselves. Fresh from a winter in the tropics, their blood filled with the chemistry of reproduction, the males seem to explode with song. Roger Tory Peterson describes their outburst as "a stuttering, gurgling song, rising in a musical burst, then falling at the end." The National Geographic Society *Field Guide* is less precise but more poetic: "an exuberant song, a cascade of bubbling whistled notes." Frank M. Chapman, one of the pioneers of American bird study, called the song "a sudden outpouring of music which completely dominates the singer, who with raised head and drooped tail trembles with the violence of his effort." Clearly the song of the house wren is a master performance. Since the wrens occupied two of our birdhouses every year, on opposite sides of our house, we became very well acquainted with the song, but we'll make no attempt to add still another description other than to call it one of the most joyous sounds of spring.

House wrens bear a particularly descriptive scientific name: *Troglodytes aedon*. A troglodyte is a cave dweller, hence one who nests in cavities such as birdhouses; *aedon* is the Greek word for a songster. Birds that depend upon cavities for nesting find the accommodations scanty. There are far more house hunters than openings—not only for wrens but for bluebirds, chickadees, nuthatches, tree and violet-green swallows, and others. House wrens often return to the same nesting site year after year, and they are aggressive in defending it from all comers. Despite their small size, they are remarkably pugnacious, telling off intruders with harsh chatter. Frank Chapman speaks of the birds' "irritable disposition," perhaps an understatement. We found that house wrens would often fill up birdhouses other than their own with sticks, right up to the entrance, presumably to discourage other birds from nesting there. On one occasion wrens displaced white-breasted nuthatches from a box just below our deck. We did not see the actual displacement and do not know if young were in the nest at the time. But the change in ownership was abrupt and final.

House wrens have been known for a long time to destroy the nests of other birds, but only recently has there been experimental evidence bearing on this unusual behavior. Two Canadian biologists, Jean-Claude Belles-Isles and Jaroslav Picman, offered thirty-eight house wrens nests with eggs of several kinds of birds, and found that the wrens consistently attacked all of them. The birds included yellow warblers, robins, quails, and house wrens. In each case, in spite of differences in size and color of the eggs and of the nature of the nests, the wrens picked the eggs and dropped them from the nest. In some cases they also removed nesting material. The experimental nests were placed several feet away from house wren nest boxes, and up to more than sixty feet away. The aggressors were both males and females that had not yet established their families.

It is easy to understand why house wrens would defend their own nest site as well as their immediate surroundings, considering the scarcity of cavities suitable for nesting. But some of the eggs they attacked in these experiments were in open nests and involved species that would never compete with house wrens for nest sites. There are actually records of more than twenty other kinds of birds whose nests are known to be attacked by house wrens, and many of them do not breed in cavities. There is no evidence that house wrens eat the contents of eggs they have picked. Perhaps by destroying the eggs of neighbors, of whatever kind, they lay claim to all the insect food near their nest. Possibly by destroying the nests of other house wrens, they may free the males and females as potential mates, for house wrens are by no means always monogamous. If this is a correct scenario, then the attacks on nests of other species would seem to result from innate ferocity. Can these small birds, harbingers of spring, really be such blackguards?

That male house wrens often seek second mates is well known. When there are other birdhouses nearby, and the first female has begun to incubate, a male will often spend part of his time at another birdhouse, singing to attract another mate. Studies in Wyoming by L. Scott Johnson and L. Henry Kermott showed that eight of fifteen males they observed succeeded in attracting a female to a second nest box. Males normally provide food to the incubating female and to the young, but they do not do so nearly so consistently for the second mate. Johnson and Kermott showed that second females usually raise fewer offspring and these are of lower quality, since the female must often have to feed herself and her nestlings.

Despite living lives that by human standards seem unsuitable for such attractive and melodious little birds, our house wrens were more than welcome as members of our community. We enjoyed watching them as they moved mouse-like, beneath bushes and fallen logs in search of insect prey. And we were amused by their courtship antics, when a male would pour forth his song from the tip of a branch while the female, below, fluttered her wings and produced a rapid series of chirps. We were dismayed to watch Steller's jays seizing nestlings from house wren boxes and flying off with them. House wrens fill up most of their boxes with twigs, then build a nest of grasses and feathers on top, just inside the entrance. So it was easy for jays to reach in. Despite their noisy complaints, wrens are too small to do much to deter jays. We eventually replaced our birdhouses with ones having a thick wooden ring outside the entrance, so that jays could not reach into the nests.

Although we had many occasions to admire our house wrens, we became particularly attached to the rock wren that each year held forth from the top of the granite promontory just west of our deck. We spoke of him as "our" rock wren, though we had no way of knowing whether it was the same male that had performed the year before, his son, or a male from elsewhere. Rock wrens are slightly larger than house wrens, have a longer bill, and lack the upturned tail. They are forever flexing their legs, as if doing "push-ups," as they sing or hop about the rocks in a search for insects. We have never found a nest, which is reported to be located in crannies among the rocks and built of sticks, with a lining of grasses, hairs, and feathers. Persons who have found nests report that the entranceway is paved with small, flat stones that the birds have gathered and placed there, for reasons unknown. In the deep Southwest, rock wrens may even use fragments of Indian pottery as part of their pavement. These wrens have a better reputation than house wrens; they are not known to cheat on their spouses or to attack the nests of other birds.

The song of the rock wren is so utterly different from that of the house wren that it is hard to believe that the two species are related. For variety it can hardly be surpassed, for there are several quite different phrases that can be presented in any order. Some are sweet and melodious (tuwee

tuwee tuwee, deedle deedle deedle) while others are harsh
(kr kr kr kr). Each phrase has three to eight repeated sylla-
bles, and a complete song consists of several different
phrases, with a brief pause between each. Sitting on our
deck, we often tried to guess which phrase would come up
next, and we wondered how the wren decided the matter.

We spotted a canyon wren only once near our house, and
recognized it by its white throat and dark lower breast, in
contrast to the streaked breast of the otherwise very similar
rock wren. We never heard it singing near our home, but we
often heard it while hiking in nearby canyons. In fact on
one hike we heard all three kinds of wrens within a few
minutes of one another, a house wren from the canyon bottom, a rock wren from a rocky slope, and a canyon wren
from atop a vertical cliff. It was a moment not to be forgot-
ten. The unique, descending clear notes of the canyon wren
are part of the mystique of every steep-walled western
canyon. Naturalist William Beebe described the song as "a
silvery dropping of eight or ten clear, sweet notes, becoming more plaintive as they descend. ... The silvery quality is
of marvelous depth and purity."

The striking differences between the songs of these three
wrens can be extended to other species. On trips to the
southeastern states, we have been treated to the loud
"cheedl, cheedl, cheedl" of the Carolina wren, and in the
deserts of the Southwest to the harsh, almost jackhammer
song of the cactus wren, the rapid notes all on the same
pitch. The winter wren, which we have heard in the forests
of the Northwest, has a rather mad, tinkling and tumbling
outburst, usually uttered from deep in damp vegetation. In
his article comparing the songs of wrens, Donald Kroodsma,
of Rockefeller University, rates the song complexity of the
winter wren as sixty-six, in terms of components included
in the song, by far the greatest of all wren species (the house

wren rates 11.5). Winter wrens also have the longest songs
and spend the most time singing.

Why are the songs of wrens so unlike one another? Donald
Kroodsma points out that wrens are small and rather plain
gray-brown in color, and males and females are colored
alike. They advertise their presence by loud and distinctive
songs. It hardly seems that such differences in song would
be needed for a wren to recognize another wren as a member of the same or a different species—especially considering the differences in habitat. Bird songs not only serve to
inform other birds that "this is my territory," but also to
bring the sexes together. Researchers have shown that if
recorded house wren songs are broadcast from empty nest
boxes, females are attracted in much greater numbers than
they are to silent boxes, and some will remain for a considerable time despite the absence of a male.

There are experiments with mockingbirds that show that
males with the most complex songs attract females earlier in
the season than males with simpler songs. Experiments with
redwinged blackbirds, which like house wrens are frequently polygynous, have shown that there is a correlation
between size of the male's song repertory and the number
of females he is able to attract. So one can imagine a time in
the early evolutionary divergence of wren species when
songs differed only sufficiently to identify the species. But
as females consistently chose males with the richest songs,
over many generations, there would be evolution in each
lineage for the development of more complex and distinctive songs. By accepting the "best" male, as judged by his
song, a female was also likely to be accepting an especially
vigorous mate who may also help to produce vigorous offspring. The male offspring are also likely to produce superior songs. Biologists believe that when superior singing
ability is at a premium, there may be unusually rapid ("run-

away") evolutionary change, producing results that may seem extreme. In the case of wrens, there seems no better way to understand such remarkable and distinctive songs, produced by small and rather monotonously colored birds.

Does it reduce a person's love of nature to ask *how* and *why* questions, when the answers involve manipulating nature? We don't think so, so long as no cruelty is involved. For a person who looks upon nature as a place for meditation, for escape from the roar of the city, or simply for recreation, it may be sufficient to ask *what* questions, or perhaps no questions at all. But there is a great deal to be gained by deeper inquiry. Here there are glimpses of how the natural world works and how it may have developed its intricate networks of causes and effects. To listen to a wren singing is to wonder: what does it mean, how did such an outpouring of beautiful sound come about? Complete answers may elude us, but the song will seem more precious for the effort.

8

The Butterfly Calendar

ON LAZY DAYS in August we often sat on our deck watching the pine whites circle about our ponderosa pines. These fragile butterflies seemed enamored of the pines as they drifted among the branches, mostly toward the tops of the trees. Since our deck overlooked a slope, we could look straight across to the treetops, each of which had a butterfly or two. These were females looking for a place to lay their eggs. Most butterflies of this group (the "whites" and "sulphurs") attack herbaceous plants—the alfalfa and cabbage butterflies belong to this group. Pine whites are unique in having larvae that feed on pine needles. It is said that they prefer older needles to new ones, a very tough diet indeed.

We were surprised to find the pine white important enough to occupy over two pages in the U.S. Forest Service's book *Western Forest Insects*, where it is stated to be "one of the most destructive insect enemies of ponderosa pine." We have never found the eggs, which are reported to be "emerald-green" and laid in a row on the needles. Nor have we ever found the green, black-headed caterpillars or noted any damage they may be doing to our pines. Yet we are told that in the Pacific Northwest the caterpillars have sometimes defoliated many acres of forest.

When pine whites arrived, the sequence of butterflies that had graced our meadows was nearly complete. In the earliest spring, even on warm days in winter, mourning cloaks were about. As soon as the willows began to leaf out they would be laying their eggs there, and soon the spiny, red-flecked caterpillars would be consuming the foliage. Smaller, orange-banded butterflies also appeared early in spring. These were Milbert's tortoiseshells, an odd name for a welcome harbinger of spring. The larvae of these butterflies feed on nettle, to which they are most welcome. The satyr anglewing, speckled orange above and leaf-like brown when the wings are closed, was also on the wing as early as April and also addicted to nettle.

These three butterflies had all overwintered as adult butterflies under bark or in some other concealed place. Soon they were joined by others that had spent the winter as pupae. One of the first of these was the silvery blue, a tiny butterfly that seemed to challenge the blue of the sky. These butterflies spent their time at early wildflowers and at the unfolding leaves of lupines and locoweeds, where the females lay their eggs. The silvery blue is a close relative of the xerces blue, a California species that is now extinct as a result of habitat destruction; it has given its name to the Xerces Society, dedicated to the preservation of invertebrates.

Another jewel of spring was the juniper hairstreak, brownish above but improbably patterned with green below, with a slender filament or "hairstreak" dangling from the hind wing. The larvae are reported to feed on the tips of junipers and to mimic the appearance of the foliage—a rough diet for so delicate a creature, one would think. In the course of the summer other hairstreaks, blues, and "coppers" appeared, coppers being adorned with reddish and coppery colors. The most elegant of these, the Colorado hairstreak, has recently been named Colorado's state insect. Unfortunately it does not occur here, since its larvae feed on Gambel oak, which ranges well to the south of us. But we did at least have four other kinds of hairstreaks, six other blues, three coppers, and two small brown "elfins."

All of these belong to the family Lycaenidae, a name apparently based on the Greek word for wolf, *lykos*. This seems an odd name for a group of small butterflies, and may have been applied because a few species have larvae that are carnivorous, feeding upon aphids and other small insects. Lycaenid larvae are plump, hairy caterpillars with retractile heads, and many of them have glands that produce a sugary substance that is attractive to ants. Ants feed at these glands and help to protect the larvae from parasites. In some cases the ants carry the caterpillars into their nests, where they pupate and even emerge as butterflies from the galleries of the ants. This is all beyond our experience, and in fact there is still a lot to be learned about these butterflies.

Soon after the first flush of spring—the mourning cloaks, anglewings, blues, and hairsteaks—some of the most striking of butterfies appeared. These were the orangetips, small white butterflies with a splash of orange on the corner of each forewing. They flew close to the ground in shady places, and seemed most active during the early morning hours. Some years we saw none at all, while in other years the local ravines were filled with them. The larvae are said to feed on plants of the mustard family, and we certainly had plenty of those, so scarcity of food is not likely to be the cause of their occasional rarity.

Orangetips belong to the same family as the pine whites, the Pieridae. Like many butterfly names, this one is based on Greek mythology. The Pieridae were the daughters of King Pierus of Macedonia who challenged the muses of Apollo, for which impudence they were changed into magpies. Other pierids that soon appeared in the fields and meadows included several other "whites" and several "sulphurs," the latter so-called for their yellow, black-bordered wings. Researchers have shown that the wings of some species reflect ultraviolet, a color visible to many insects and believed to play an important role in courtship.

Some time in spring the first painted ladies appeared, migrants from the south and in search of thistles on which to lay their eggs. These are among the most widespread of all butterflies, occurring throughout the warmer parts of the globe. Painted ladies that reach temperate zones will have two or more broods here, but butterflies of the final brood will perish in the fall, as theirs is a one-way migration.

In bright days in May the first of the satyrs, or wood nymphs, appeared (again, names taken from mythology). These are small butterflies of modest colors, shades of brown and ocher, with circular, contrasting spots on the wings. Satyrs are weak flyers but not easy to catch as they descend into the grasses and bushes. One of the first to appear was the ocher ringlet, a pale yellow-brown species with an "eye spot" on each front wing. These delicate insects have a remarkable range, occurring throughout the northern parts of Eurasia as well as North America. Soon the ocher ringlet was joined by two other satyrs of northern distribution, with names that suggest their addiction to a cool climate: Uhler's arctic and the common alpine. Both range well north of the Arctic Circle and up to twelve thousand feet in our mountains. All of the satyrs have larvae that feed on grasses, where they are rarely spotted except by persons whose eyes are glued to the ground.

(Note that all butterflies have vernacular names, reflecting their popularity with collectors. It would be awkward and unnecessary to invent vernacular names for all the hundreds of thousands of other insects, many of which are known only to specialists. So it is still necessary to use scientific names for most of them.)

In June moderately large white butterflies appeared, flying over the meadows in a fluttering, moth-like manner, now and then landing on a flower with their wings extended, revealing black splotches and circular red spots on the wings, as if touched here and there by a watercolorist. These were parnassians, more specifically *Parnassius phoebus* (Greek mythology again!), our only member of this unique group. They had emerged from silken cocoons more like those of moths than the naked chrysalides of butterflies. Their bodies are clothed rather densely with hairlike scales, as if to keep them warm. In fact these are remarkably cold-adapted insects, ranging north into Alaska and across Siberia to northern Europe. In the Rockies they occur up to fourteen thousand feet elevation, well above timberline. We felt fortunate to have had them at a mere seventy-eight hundred feet and rejoiced when we spotted the first one crossing our meadows. The larvae feed on stonecrop sedum, one of our commonest wildflowers. We often looked for them but never found them.

June is also the month of those most regal of butterflies, the swallowtails. Situated as we were on the crest of a hill, we saw many of them gliding by. "Hilltopping" is common among many insects that gather at prominent landmarks in their search for mates. The bold black-on-yellow patterns of several species give them the name "tigers." We had the western tiger swallowtail, the pale tiger, and the two-tailed tiger, all of which lay their eggs on diverse trees. The anise and black swallowtails, on the other hand, are attracted to members of the carrot family. Larvae of all swallowtails are seemingly fearsome creatures, having extensible, orange "horns" that produce a nauseous odor. In fact it is butyric acid, similar to that produced by rancid butter. Tiger swallowtail caterpillars also have a pair of prominent "eye spots" near the front of the body, each no more than a black spot rimmed with yellow, but presumably sufficiently eyelike to cause birds to hesitate before seizing them.

Swallowtails, and pierids, too, often gather at damp soil, behavior usually described as "puddling." Here they uncoil their long tongues and insert them into the soil to extract sodium and other minerals. Butterflies seen puddling are most often young males, and in at least some cases the males transfer sodium to the females at the time of mating, sodium being important for egg production. Older females may puddle to replenish their sodium when they have mated some time ago. Not that they "decide" to do so, in the way that we consume dietary supplements, but presumably they experience a hunger for the rewards of mud. We well remember hikes on tropical trails, when great clouds of butterflies flew up from the damp soil and surrounded us. Butterflies also sometimes come to the droppings of mammals for similar reasons.

July is the month of fritillaries, medium to large orange butterflies with wings speckled with black and, on the under side, often spotted with silver. *Fritillus* is Latin for a dice box, hence spotted like dice. These are butterflies of full summer, imbibing nectar at thistles, pink bergamot, and other summer flowers. We had five relatively large species, not easily told apart unless we caught them and took them to our field guide. The larvae are reported to feed on violets. This seemed curious to us, since violets were not especially abundant locally (though we had several species). Fritillaries, however, seemed to be with us in numbers every summer, among our most conspicuous and reliable butterflies.

Fritillaries have smaller cousins, called checkerspots, also mostly orange and black-speckled. We had four common species, and probably others we hadn't properly distinguished. Again, they derive their scientific name from mythology: *Euphydryas*, Greek for "graceful nymph." Many checkerspot species select members of the figwort family (such as penstemon and Indian paintbrush) on which to lay their eggs. Members of this group of plants contain substances called iridoid glycosides, which are poisonous to most animals, but serve as feeding stimulants for checkerspot larvae. The larvae sequester these substances through the pupal stage into the adult butterflies, which advertize their unpalatability by their speckled orange coloration. Using jays as test animals, Deane Bowers, of the University of Colorado, showed that caged, trained birds learn to reject checkerspots on the basis of their content of glycosides. However, when the checkerspot larvae are fed on plantain in the laboratory, the resulting adults are accepted by jays.

By August the pine whites are out, and the first monarchs are passing through on the way to wintering sites in Mexico—or did ours go to sites along the California coast? These are tough butterflies, able to travel many miles, with occasional refueling at flowers along the way. That monarch larvae sequester poisonous alkaloids from milkweeds and pass them on to the adults has been known for some years. That monarchs are less plentiful than they once were reflects declining stands of milkweeds as we practice "clean culture" and the further paving over of our world. But especially it reflects the decimation of wintering sites in the mountains of Mexico or on the coast of California.

Winter comes, and summer's butterflies are golden memories unless one wanders to the tropics, as we sometimes did. In writing about butterflies in *Life on a Little-Known Planet* (1968), we remarked that some time we would like "to meet in person the grandest butterfly of all, the Ornithoptera, or bird-wing, of the East Indies." Since then we have camped in a melaleuca forest in extreme northeast Australia, where bird-wings coasted in numbers on their broad, splendid wings. Bird-wings are now protected by law, as they should be. Collectors wishing to enrich their holdings or, more often, marketing rare or especially beautiful butterflies to

hobbyists, have depleted butterfly populations throughout
the world. Butterflies (especially tropical ones) are being
"farmed"—to supply the butterfly pavilions that have
arisen in many places. Perhaps this will create a greater
awareness of butterflies, but we would hate to think that
some day people will have to visit butterfly houses to see
them, just as now we must visit zoos to see many of the
world's vanishing mammals.

We delighted in the butterflies that graced our fields and
meadows. Colorado has a richer butterfly fauna than many
other states, and we experienced only a small sample. Numbers of individual species vary from year to year, and some,
like the monarch, seem progressively less common. Across
the country, local populations are declining in numbers. As
of 1989, ten North American butterfly species or subspecies
were listed as threatened or endangered, while more than
twenty others were under consideration for listing. A world
increasingly overpopulated by our own species can evidently allow little space for butterflies.

A male mountain bluebird perches on our deck rail on a bright April day. (Chapter 1)

Cassin's finches perch on top of a Douglas-fir just beyond our deck. (Chapter 1)

The nest of thatcher ants, built against a log, covered with twigs and needles to a depth of several inches. (Chapter 2)

A worker thatcher ant grasps a Douglas-fir needle as she works on the roof of the nest. (Chapter 2)

A female *Podalonia luctuosa* digger wasp carries a cutworm caterpillar to her nest. (Chapter 4)

A long-tailed weasel in its winter coat is about to take suet from one of our feeders. (Chapter 1)

A male broad-tailed hummingbird perches at a feeder. (Chapter 3)

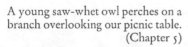

A young saw-whet owl perches on a branch overlooking our picnic table. (Chapter 5)

Many of the "blues" have the underside of their wings speckled. This is the Rocky Mountain dotted blue, *Euphilotes ancilla*. (Chapter 8)

A male pale western swallowtail "puddling," extending his tongue into the soil, imbibing minerals. (Chapter 8)

In late summer, the flowers of rabbit brush attract many insects. This freshly emerged painted lady will not survive the coming frosts. (Chapter 8)

A male bumblebee on his territorial perch, his antennae extended stiffly forward. (Chapter 6)

A tassel-eared squirrel stands on a rock outside our windows, displaying his long winter ear tufts. (Chapter 9)

A Clark's nutcracker in a tranquil pose. (Chapter 13) (*photograph by David Leatherman*)

Pasque flowers spring up in early spring, before the hummingbirds have arrived and while few bees are about. (Chapter 12)

The unusual beak of
a red crossbill.
(Chapter 15)
*(photograph by
David Leatherman)*

A mating pair of beewolves, the female on
the left. This is *Philanthus pulcher*, one of
four species that occurred near our home.
(Chapter 16)

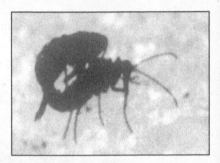

A mating pair of wingless scorpion flies
on a snowdrift, the female above the male.
This may be the first photograph of these
very small insects mating. (Chapter 10)

A female pollen wasp at the flowers
of a one-sided penstemmon.
(Chapter 14)

Shooting-star primroses grew in wet places along the trail, often in great numbers. (Chapter 17)

Coral-root orchids grew along the trail each year, rising from clumps of decaying organic matter. (Chapter 17)

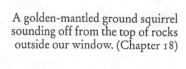

A golden-mantled ground squirrel sounding off from the top of rocks outside our window. (Chapter 18)

A rock squirrel visited us just once during our years in the mountains. (Chapter 18)

A caterpillar of an agapema silkmoth that has defoliated a squaw currant bush. (Chapter 19)

A marmot sunning itself on top of rocks beyond our deck. (Chapter 18)

The berries of skunkbrush, a shrub that graced many of the meadows and hillsides near our home. (Chapter 19)

9

A Squirrel Like No Other

ONE OF THE MOST common visitors at our mountain home was a beautiful animal known only to persons who live or camp in the belt of ponderosa pines at moderate elevations along the Rockies. This is the tassel-eared (or Abert's) squirrel. At first glance, the squirrels seem hardly believable. Why should they grow long hairs on their ears in winter; do they keep their ears warm? Why do they sport solid deep brown to black fur, even on snowy landscapes, when weasels and snowshoe hares have turned white? Why are some individuals, even littermates, not dark in color at all, but gray above and white below, with a dark stripe along the side? And why is their diet restricted to just one plant (ponderosa pine), restricted feeding behavior more like a koala than nearly all other mammals? None of these questions are easily answered.

In his book *Rocky Mountain Mammals*, David Armstrong remarks that a person who sees this mammal "ought to consider the day well spent." Many of our days were well spent, as the squirrels appeared on our deck regularly in winter, disposing of any sunflower seeds that had fallen from our feeder, or any that we had placed on the floor especially for them. We called them "blackies," despite the fact that they were really very deep brown. There were sometimes two at a time, resulting in a bit of a scramble. We learned to recognize individuals through differences in their tails. Only rarely did a gray and white individual appear.

Tassel-eared squirrels are unknown outside their limited range, from extreme southern Wyoming to mountainous parts of New Mexico and Arizona, only in a narrow belt of suitable, open forests. Early explorers in the Rockies were unfamiliar with the squirrels. Lewis and Clark were too far north, and Zebulon Pike, though he spent time well within the squirrel's range, was by his own admission not much of a naturalist. The Long Expedition of 1820 had trained naturalists, and zoologist Thomas Say described and named the rock squirrel, the golden-mantled ground squirrel, and the Colorado chipmunk. But he failed to find the tassel-eared squirrel. J.C. Frémont trekked well within the range on his second expedition, in 1843, but did not report the squirrels, nor did he on his third and fourth expeditions, in 1845 and 1848.

It remained for army physician Samuel Woodhouse, an enthusiastic naturalist, to discover and describe the squirrels from the San Francisco Peaks of Arizona in 1851. Woodhouse was a member of the army's Zuni River Expedition, and he had a rough time of it; he was bitten by a rattlesnake and later pierced by the arrow of a Yavapai Indian. But he came home with a fine collection of specimens. He named the squirrel after his commanding officer, Colonel J.J. Abert, chief of the Army Topographic Engineers. Nowadays it is more often called the tassel-eared squirrel, even though the "tassels" are lost during the summer, when these elegant rodents are most often seen by travelers in the mountains.

The squirrels are closely associated with ponderosa pines, feeding in the spring on apical buds and staminate flowers, in summer and fall on seeds they dissect from the cones. In winter, when little else is available, they feed on the inner bark of terminal twigs. There is evidence that they are able to select certain trees as food to the exclusion of many others. In an article in the magazine *Natural History* in 1993, Marc Snyder and Yan Linhart described how the squirrels gnaw off a shoot, then sever the terminal needles, which fall to the ground. Then they hold the section in their paws, scrape off the outer bark, and feed on the inner bark. As they do this, there begins a flow of resin containing terpenes and other substances that pines have evolved in their own defense. Through a series of ingenious experiments, Snyder and Linhart showed that squirrels prefer trees that produce resin slowly and resin that contains fewer unpleasant chemicals. They fed squirrels peanut butter, either straight or laced with terpenes in various concentrations. They much preferred plain peanut butter. They also showed that tassel-eared squirrels prefer trees high in carbohydrates and sodium and avoid those containing high levels of iron or mercury. Having located trees having the most desirable food quality, the squirrels return again and again, sometimes doing considerable damage to the trees. Perhaps the fact that the squirrels vary so much in time and space permits pines to recover before damage is extreme. Sometimes the squirrels collect mushrooms and will even store them for a time, although most foods are not cached. We have seen them nibble on mistletoe, a common parasite of ponderosa pines, and wished they might be more persistent in attacking those pestiferous plants. But an occasional nibble at a mushroom or mistletoe, or a snack of sunflower seeds, does not represent much of a departure from their devotion to ponderosa pines as food.

When a tassel-eared squirrel arrived on our deck, any birds feeding on the floor absconded, and so did chipmunks and ground squirrels. But red squirrels (pine squirrels in local parlance) were not always easily displaced. They are less than half the size of the tassel-ears, averaging about two hundred grams as compared to about seven hundred grams for the tassel-ears. But they are twice as feisty, and occasionally chased away one of the more timid tassel-ears (though sometimes the reverse was true). Red squirrels, in the Rockies, are more characteristic of lodgepole pine forests, found a bit higher in the mountains. But these abundant animals sometimes range into ponderosa forests, where they doubtless compete with the tassel-ears to a degree.

Although tassel-eared squirrels are quiet and undemonstrative animals most of the time, they do (like all animals) have ways of communicating and of displaying their emotions. Tail flicking, foot stomping, tooth chattering, and alarm barks are all ways of announcing their mood. On our deck, individuals would sometimes spread themselves and lie flat on their bellies for a time, as if enjoying the sun or a cessation of the continual search for food. The squirrels are solitary animals through much of the year, each having a home range of about twenty acres. They do not defend a territory, however, and home ranges may overlap. Robert Farentinos live-trapped squirrels in the mountains west of Boulder, Colorado. Before releasing them he marked each one with "Lady Clairol Ultra Blue," not to enhance their charm but to lighten their fur in patterns so they could be recognized individually. When squirrels meet in a feeding tree, a pursuit may follow, with much chattering. During the mating season, in early spring, both males and females become more aggressive, and males in pursuit of a female in estrus tend to form a dominance hierarchy, the dominant male attempting to monopolize the female and drive away other males. Females are not easily seduced; they use threatening displays and much angry chatter toward the male. Following a mating chase that may last several hours, the female finally becomes receptive and allows the male to mount. No doubt some of the shenanigans that went on our deck were parts of mating chases, but we were quite unable to tell a male from a female.

We never found a nest, but learned that they are built fifteen to thirty feet high in large pine trees. Robert Farentinos found two types of nests. Bolus nests are built of pine twigs in the form of a ball two or three feet in diameter, usually where a major limb meets the trunk. Inside they are lined with grasses and other soft materials. The squirrels are not above snatching nest linings from homes, as we discovered when we left our kitchen mop on the deck railing to dry. Broom nests are built inside "witches' brooms" formed by trees in response to infestation by mistletoe; the dense twigs form a supporting frame for the nest. Nests are used throughout the year. Young are born there in June or July, two to five to a litter. By late summer the young leave the nest and are on their own.

Populations fluctuate from year to year, as they do in many mammals. But so far tassel-eared squirrels seem to be adjusting to the increased presence of people in their habitat. At least "our" squirrels accepted our hospitality, even though they sputtered angrily if we tried to achieve greater intimacy. Like so many animals, they often cross roads in front of cars. Now that so many roads and four-wheel drive tracks penetrate our forests, the squirrels may have to struggle to maintain their numbers. We wish them well.

10

A Society of Flies

THE THIRD WEEK IN June was the time of a special event
in our area, a bit of excitement that passed unnoticed except
by a privileged few. It was the time of appearance of *Rhamphomyia sociabilis*, a wonderful fly with a wonderful name
(*Rhamphomyia* is Greek for beak-fly, *sociabilis* Latin that
needs no translation). For many months these insects were
small, worm-like creatures living in rotting organic matter
in the soil. Then, as if they had a calendar, they appear in
swarms and go about the job of producing a new generation
of themselves. In 1986 they appeared on June 16, in 1987
and 1988 on June 19, in 1989 on June 20. We followed them
for thirteen years. Each year they appeared on about the
same date and remained active for about a month (although
in 1990 they were present up to August 26, perhaps having
produced a second generation that year).

Remarkably, they always appeared in the same places.
One of these places was in the walkway leading to our house,
an aisle about five by twenty yards with tall ponderosa
pines and Douglas-firs on each side. Here they were especially easy to observe and hardly at all disturbed by our use
of the path; they seemed to be insisting that we study them.
We were careful to keep our mouths closed as we walked up
the path. Not that swallowing a few flies would hurt us.
These are not the blue-tailed flies, fresh from a carcass, that

Burl Ives used to sing about, but "dance flies," a name meant to describe their yearly propensity to spend a few days in aerial gamboling.

Another swarm formed on much the same dates in a space among pine trees about a quarter of a mile away, a third one in a similar habitat about five miles away. Not only did the flies seem to "know" when to appear, but where to gather and perform. Each of the sites was just northeast of a rocky promontory, so that to some degree they were protected from the prevailing southwesterly winds of summer. We explored many similar sites in the area, but found swarms on only these three places. Winds did toss them about a bit, and a stiff wind caused them to disperse. The flies were not disturbed by a light rain, but they disappeared during a heavy rain.

These are tiny flies, a bit less than a quarter of an inch long, and one would hardly notice them individually. But when a dozen to more than a hundred gather at one site they are quite noticeable, and even produce an audible hum if many are active and there are no other noises at the time. They appeared each day from one to six feet above the ground (usually two to four feet), drifting about in a more or less circular cloud in the partial shade. Within the swarm, each fly moved in circles, figure eights, or irregular patterns, hardly ever bumping into another fly.

On pleasant days the flies appeared an hour or two after sunrise and formed a rather diffuse swarm in which individuals drifted slowly about. When we captured some of them in an insect net we found that all were males and each was holding a very small insect it had captured before joining the swarm. Soon there were other flies passing back and forth rapidly beside the swarm, and a sweep net of these flies showed them all to be females. One by one the females joined the swarm, each one approaching a male from below and taking the small prey that the male had captured. Having lured a female, the male mated with her while she inserted her beak into the prey and sucked out its body fluids. Females probably take no other food except for that supplied by her partner; they may well have lost the ability to hunt for themselves.

By mid-morning the swarm was quite conspicuous, as each unit was a triad, the male above holding the female below, the female feeding on a small gift from the male. We found it difficult to follow individual pairs, even when we dusted them with flour. Apparently mating is completed in flight and takes only a few minutes. It may well be that the duration of mating depends upon the size of the prey the male has provided to the female.

This is the time of year when hummingbirds are feeding their young, and we often saw hummingbirds hovering and snatching flies as they drifted about in the swarm. By late morning, many of the flies have dispersed, the females presumably to lay their eggs, the males to hunt more prey. On warm days there were few if any flies swarming at mid-day, but in the afternoon they had gathered again and performed right up to sundown.

Females appeared to accept whatever prey the male presented. Most commonly it was a very small fly, such as a fruit fly or a blackfly. Leafhoppers also served well, as did small, winged ants. In all, we found insects of six orders to be used as prey, even including a mayfly and a small moth. Other species of dance flies sometimes also served as prey, but the males seemed to avoid preying on members of their own species.

Flies that swarm usually do so over a particular "marker," often a bush, a stream, or a dark place on the ground. Or it may be an arena between markers, as in the case of "our" flies. One year someone cut down a large pine that bordered one of the spaces occupied by a swarm that we had been watching. The flies never reappeared there. When markers remain constant, flies of successive generations return to the same place. Encoded in their genes, we assume, is a "picture" of their traditional swarm site.

Males and females are easy to tell apart, as the females are ornamented with large scales along their legs. In insects (as in birds) it is usually the males that are more highly ornamented and prepared to display before the females. In dance flies, the females compete for males, who are ready to supply them with a meal. Perhaps the males accept females that display their leg fringes especially well, and perhaps the females select a mate with a particularly choice bit of prey. It would take a great deal of very careful research to find out if these surmises are correct.

Females of a species of *Rhamphomyia* dance fly common in the eastern states inflate the sides of their abdomens with air so that they resemble small balloons; in fact they collapse if they are punctured. Perhaps the air sacs enable the females to drift about on air currents more readily. But David Funk, who studied these flies in Pennsylvania, designed models of flies of different sizes and found that males prefer the "plumpest" females. So it may be that the major function of the air sacs is to attract a mate.

Perhaps the most remarkable example of female adornment has been described by B.G. Svensson, working in Sweden on a different species of this same genus. These flies also swarm in clearings among trees, and the same swarm sites are used on several successive summers. Although the males are unremarkable, the females have fan-shaped wings of nearly twice the surface area of the wings of the males. Furthermore, while the wings of the males are clear, those of the females have a dark band on the outer half. In both this species and the preceding, swarms initially consist of females, and males fly in carrying prey. The males presumably select a particularly "good" female on the basis of her display, an example of "sex reversal," since it is usually the female that does the choosing on the basis of male adornments.

In some other species of dance flies, males are known to present females with prey that has been used before and sucked dry. In some instances, wind-blown seeds of willows or poplars are presented and apparently accepted as "prey." An amateur entomologist, A.H. Hamm, once watched some dance flies along a stream in the English countryside. He saw the males picking up bright objects from the surface of the water, either insects or pieces of leaves or flowers. He threw petals of buttercups onto the water, and the flies picked them up and carried them like banners, finally passing them to the females during mating.

There is a species of dance fly in which males wrap their prey in silken threads, and still another in which males form a sphere of bubbles in which the prey is imbedded. More astonishing is the fact that males of some species present a glistening ball of secretions containing no prey at all. The female holds this ball during mating, even though the male has presented her with a bauble of no value as food. Evidently such nuptial gifts have evolved into visual signals that release reproductive behavior, even though the female obtains no nutrients. It is difficult not to make a comparison with human courtship. Would the lady prefer a box of candy or a glistening earring?

If females have lost the ability to capture prey, how do they survive and lay eggs if the male has provided them with something inedible? Perhaps they have evolved "autogenous behavior," as occurs in some mosquitoes and other flies. That is, they retain enough body fat from their larval stage to enable them to lay eggs without feeding as adults.

Dance flies are not the only insects in which the males present the females with a "gift," inducing her to mate. Randy Thornhill, of the University of New Mexico, has spent many years observing hanging-flies, members of quite a different order of insects called scorpion flies. Male hanging flies capture prey and suspend themselves in vegetation by their long legs. They have an additional "gimmick," a gland that produces an odor that attracts females from a distance. When a female arrives, she evaluates the prey for size and edibility (lady beetles, for example, won't do, as their blood is very bitter). If the prey is large and edible, the female may feed on it for half an hour or more while she mates with the male.

In another kind of scorpion fly, called *Panorpa*, males "prey" on dead insects, which they often pick up from spider's webs. Females readily accept these nuptial gifts, though preferring larger ones to smaller ones. Males that are unable to find a dead insect may simply regurgitate a lump of saliva onto a leaf, then stand by the secretions and produce a volatile attractant from special glands. I have had no opportunity to see these goings-on, as scorpion flies do not thrive in our semiarid landscape. Thornhill's studies were done in Virginia and Michigan.

Some day soon we hope to revisit our former haunts on a pleasant day between mid-June and mid-July, simply to reassure ourselves that our flies are still performing. Living as we do in a society that is in constant flux and addicted to growth and "progress," it is refreshing to stay in touch with rhythms of nature that persist through time. Doubtless the flies will still be "dancing" long after we are gone, and probably long after our species has joined the dinosaurs in extinction.

II

Woodrats

WOODRATS ARE ABUNDANT animals in rural and wild country, especially if the terrain is rocky and (as their name implies) wooded. We should have expected them when we built a home on a rocky ledge among pines and Douglas-firs. But this was a new habitat for us, and we had no idea that some of the local fauna would consider our house just a novel arrangement of timber suitable, in fact very desirable, for habitation. Woodrats were intermittent houseguests for all of our thirteen years there.

These are very different animals from the Norway rats that inhabit the back alleys and garbage dumps of the cities. Woodrats are natives, not aliens, and altogether more attractive animals, soft-furred, hairy-tailed, and living off the land without depleting it in any important way. Since they are nocturnal, they are rarely noticed unless people make a home in a place woodrats have occupied for many years, as we did. Nights were usually very quiet at our home: no traffic sounds, no sirens, no voices in the night except now and then owls or coyotes. But far too often there was scuffling beneath the floors, and the sounds of gnawing on wood and electric wires. Despite our enjoyment of our wild neighbors, we did not appreciate having our sleep interrupted. Nor did we care to pay an electrician to replace our wires every once in a while. So despite our admiration for the adaptability of woodrats, and our admission of the fact that they had no doubt lived here long before we arrived, our relations were not the best.

At first we were merely puzzled by the goings-on under the floors. Then, one night, we searched with our flashlights and discovered a bushy tail hanging from a hole in the ceiling of our downstairs utility room. This led us to buy a live trap, which we set out and baited with lettuce. Bushy-tailed woodrats (*Neotoma cinerea*) proved very easy to trap, and over time we took several and released them a mile or two away. They were attractive animals, soft gray-buff above and white below, with big eyes and ears and a bushy, almost squirrel-like tail. Adults were about a foot long, a third of that tail. They seemed gentle creatures, lovable enough if one could learn to sleep through their nightly shenanigans.

After making the acquaintance of the bushy-tailed woodrat, we turned to our books and discovered that they range from Colorado and California all the way north to the Yukon, and in altitude from the ponderosa pine zone up to alpine talus slopes. These are the packrats of the West, notorious for collecting all kinds of trash to augment their nests. Once we learned this, we studied the crawl space beneath the house, and sure enough, there was a trail of sticks and bits of leaves leading to the enclosed space beneath our water heater and sewage retention tank. When we removed the boards to get into the space, we found a great heap of material, including wads of the insulation from our house, lots of sticks and leaves, pine needles, bones, a pencil, and a small piece of plastic. Removing all of this was a chore, as there were pieces of prickly-pear cactus all through it.

In his book *Rocky Mountain Mammals*, David Armstrong lists the following catalog of several Colorado dens: "tarpaper, nails, rattlesnake carcass, peach pit, snakeskin, rope, leather glove, shotgun shell, coal, bolt (and spare nut), hacksaw blade, wire, porcelain insulator, sticks, stones, and dung." Individual packrats take advantage of items available to them. Robert Finley, author of *The Wood Rats of Colorado*, reported a den in a cave, where there were many bones of animals that had lived there or had been brought there by predators. The bones included those of bear, badger, cat, deer, sheep, porcupine, goose, grouse, and woodrat. Also in or about the den were stones, pieces of broken bottles, pine cones, and a mummified chipmunk. Perhaps the best-known account of a packrat's collection is that of Theodore Roosevelt, who found a den at his ranch in South Dakota. He reported "a small revolver, a hunting knife, two books, a fork, a small bag, and a tin cup."

Packrats often inhabited the cabins of hunters and prospectors in the West, and there are many tales of their thievery. Some called them "trade rats" and claimed that if they took an object they would replace it with another. David Armstrong points out that packrats do sometimes leave one object and take another, but "from limited cargo capacity and not from some innate sense of fair play."

Away from human habitation, bushy-tailed woodrats build their "houses" among rocks, in caves, or in tree cavities. Their food consists of cuttings of many different kinds of trees and shrubs, even the needles of conifers, less often of whatever berries or nuts are available nearby. Oddly, they have little taste for sage, even though sagebrush is often plentiful within their habitat.

In late summer and fall large amounts of plant material are stored as food, for woodrats do not hibernate. Foliage is allowed to dry before being packed into the nest area. Robert Finley found one nest that contained more than a gallon of foliage from Douglas-fir, another that had eighty-eight dried mushrooms. Something of what goes on with respect to food storage can be discovered by inducing woodrats to nest in artificial nests that can be taken apart and their contents analyzed. This has been done by Eva Horne and her colleagues at Kansas State University, with respect to a different species, the eastern woodrat. They replaced natural houses with ones made of cut-off metal drums in which they placed plastic buckets that could be removed periodically and the contents studied. The wood-rats accepted these nests and used the buckets for storage. Caches included leaves, seeds, nuts, and bone, as well as more inedible objects. Winter stocks weighed about a thou-sand grams (dry weight), valued at about sixty-eight hun-dred kilocalories. These were reduced by spring to about four hundred grams, valued at about twenty-five hundred kilocalories.

Inside or close beside a more or less massive "house" is the nest proper; a cup-shaped structure lined with shredded bark, plant fibers, moss, and animal hairs. If the nest is near a human habitation, string and bits of cloth may be used. Within the nest a litter of two to four young (rarely up to six) is produced in spring. Harold Egoscue, of the Univer-sity of Utah, found bushy-tailed woodrats easy to rear and tame enough that he could watch them closely. Males have a scent gland on their underside that produces a musky sub-stance that is applied to nearby objects, marking their terri-tory. When a pair is ready to mate, the male follows the female about while making a low buzzing sound. In the laboratory, mating goes on all through the year, and several litters are produced.

Other sounds produced by woodrats include tail rattlings, made by flapping the tail vigorously against sticks and other nearby objects. These are believed to be alarm or aggressive signals. Woodrats also have a variety of squeals, produced especially when an unwelcome woodrat approaches them too closely. Woodrats are relatively clean animals, keeping the nest

clear of excrement and leaving the nest to urinate. They sometimes bathe in dust or loose earth when they can find it.

We have not mentioned to this point that we had a second kind of woodrat performing under our floors. These
were Mexican woodrats, here at the northern extremity of
a range that extends well into Mexico. Since there are nine
species of woodrats in the United States, we were privileged to have 22 percent of the fauna in our home. We did
not often think of it as a privilege, though the animals did
provide a certain amount of entertainment as well as an
opportunity to compare two related but rather different
species. Mexican woodrats are less attractive than bushy-
tails; they have smaller ears and a tail that is hairy but not
really bushy. We found them noisier than bushy-tails, forever pattering beneath our kitchen floor and gnawing on
wood, usually in the middle of the night. Evidently they
were trying to widen their entryways into favorite places.

They also seemed more intelligent than bushy-tails. At
least they were harder to catch in live traps, and we often
had to resort to ordinary, spring-type rat traps, which of
course killed them. Evidently they had established an odor
trail from outside the house to spaces under the floor.
Each year, in late summer, we had an invasion; one year we
trapped fourteen! Many of these were juveniles, which
had probably been forced from their parental nests.
Repeated efforts to find their point of entry failed. We had
been outsmarted by a rodent, and won the battle only by
being cruel to the point that it bothered us a good deal.

Mexican woodrats are not really packrats. They have at
most a weak inclination to collect odds and ends to fill their
dens, although their dens of sticks may contain bones, feathers, stones, and pine cones. Usually they nest among rocks,
and like other woodrats they store food for the winter.
We have no evidence that they ever built a nest in our house.

We usually caught them within a day or two after they entered, so they would have had little time to build. Their food is reported to differ only slightly from that of bushy-tails. Evidently they have less taste for cacti but considerable taste for yucca despite the tough leaves of the latter ("Spanish bayonets"). We often saw yucca plants near our home in which the leaves had been chewed to the ground, and we suspected that Mexican woodrats had been at work.

Mexican woodrats are reported to have two or three litters a year, with two to four young per litter. Females are said to be ready to mate within a couple of months after birth. So it is not surprising that they were able to invade our house quite regularly.

Both the bushy-tailed and the Mexican woodrats have plenty of parasites: lice, fleas, and ticks. The most noteworthy of these is the Rocky Mountain wood tick. These ticks have a two-year life cycle, the very small ones spending the first year on small mammals, the mature ticks spending the next year on larger mammals such as deer and humans. They are known to transmit tick fever and Rocky Mountain spotted fever, two rather uncommon diseases of humans, but they are not known to transmit Lyme disease. Primarily they are a big nuisance to people who live or hike in the woods and in bushy country in the spring. No doubt the woodrats find them equally annoying, but they are less able to remove them than we are. Perhaps we may never enter the world of woodrats in any real sense, but at least we share their parasites.

There is still much to be learned about the behavior of these small, nocturnal animals. Perhaps if we had been more patient with them we might have been able to add a few details. Woodrats may have less charm than squirrels and chipmunks, but they are very successful inhabitants of wild and rugged terrain. They deserve a good press.

12

A Curious Way to
Spend a Summer Day

WE NEVER KEPT a dog, as a dog would have been a deterrent to the wildlife we enjoyed around our house. But dogs
of neighbors did come by to check out our compost pit for
any choice items we may have discarded. Of course they left
behind occasional evidences of their presence. This was a
source of annoyance until we discovered that, in late summer, attractive little wasps were visiting dog scats on a regu-
lar basis. The wasps proved to belong to a little-studied
species, *Mellinus rufinodus*. The name might be roughly
translated "red-humped honey wasp," though animal droppings would seem a far cry from honey. Probably Johann
Fabricius, who named them in 1790, had no idea that these
wasps were such eccentrics.

No matter, these are handsome wasps, black with a spat-
tering of yellow and red bands and spots. Every year they
appeared in mid-August and were active until the first heavy
frosts. Since these are small wasps, about four-tenths of an
inch in length, any effort to study them required lying on the
ground for long periods close to dog droppings, equipped
with a notebook, magnifying glass, and sometimes even a
cup of coffee. Fortunately there were no close neighbors to
discover us occupied in such a freakish manner.

It proved a worthwhile exercise, if rather an odorous way to add a few previously unknown (unneeded?) facts to the sum of human knowledge. What attracted these wasps to such unlikely places, and what were they doing there? A little study showed that each dung pad was occupied by a single male, who perched with his antennae rigidly forward and upward, occasionally walking about with his antennae in motion. Other males often lurked nearby, but if one of them approached the dung pad he was driven off by the resident. Now and then the resident would drive off a fly or an ant. We marked several of the males with spots of paint, hoping to learn how long a male would defend a dung pad. Usually one would remain resident for most of the day, and some returned to the same site for up to five days. However, there was variation in the status of males; a male dominant one day might be driven off by a different male the next day.

Now and then a female arrived, causing the resident male to become very alert and to follow her closely. Without preliminaries, a male would leap on top of a female, grasping her with his mandibles and all three pairs of legs. Often a female would walk about with a male on her back. Now and then the two would make contact with their genitalia, and the male would then assume a semierect posture. Sometimes a pair remained together for several minutes, copulating several times. Individual males mated repeatedly, one of them eleven times in thirty minutes, probably with several different females (we did not mark the females, so this is merely a guess).

The reason for the attraction of the females to the dung was soon apparent. These wasps are attracted to the small flies that visit animal droppings. Landing near a dung pad, a female (unless harassed by a male) would walk up to a fly and suddenly pounce, rather like a cat stalking a mouse.

Females sometimes ate a fly directly, but more often they stung the fly, grasped it in their mandibles, and flew off toward their nest. Very tiny flies, as well as large "blue bottles," were ignored, but there were plenty of medium-sized flies to serve as prey.

Male insects tend to seek out places where females can be expected, either at nest sites or food sources, or sometimes (when neither is predictable) at prominent landmarks. *Mellinus* males clearly came to a food source, each male defending a site and mating with females as they arrived. To a human observer, the males seemed a source of annoyance to the females; some were harassed to the extent that they flew away without taking a fly.

For a time we speculated that the wasps might be attracted to dung by its odor, and that all hunting and mating occurred there. Later we saw both males and females on thistles that were infested with honeydew-bearing aphids. Honeydew attracts a great many insects, including ants, wasps, and flies, which imbibe the sweets. In this case it was clear that *Mellinus* females were after flies, not sweets, and the males were after the females. We saw several matings, and several times saw females flying off with their captive flies.

Females taking flies both from dung and from thistles flew off in a southwesterly direction, but they flew too swiftly and too far for us to follow. We spent endless hours over several different years searching the countryside for nests, but never found any. A European species of the same genus is reported to make deep nests in sandy soil, so we looked for eroded slopes, alluvial fans, and other such places where the wasps might nest; but to no avail. The nests of this species, as of all four of the North American species of this genus, remain undiscovered—a challenge for future generations of insect-watchers.

Europeans have done a better job of studying a species of *Mellinus* that is evidently more common than any of ours. As early as 1747, René-Antoine Ferchault de Réaumur noted the wasps provisioning their nests with flies, and since then many others have studied the wasps. Réaumur was a remarkable scientist, a noted physicist, physiologist, and mathematician, also the author of a major treatise on metallurgy and one of the discoverers of the art of steel making. Yet he had time to seek out the smallest of living things, and he left behind six (of a projected ten) volumes of his *History of Insects*. Those who knew Réaumur spoke of his "sweetness of disposition" and his "excellence of heart." The study of insects surely teaches awe and humility as well as such a dedication to the subject that there is little time to clash with fellow humans.

The European *Mellinus* also seeks out animal droppings as a source of flies, but like our species they also take flies on plants. The nests are a foot or more deep and contain several cells, each provided with four to nine paralyzed flies. The amateur entomologist A.H. Hamm, whom we met in the chapter on dance flies (with his colleague O.W. Richards), compiled a list of two hundred five flies, of many different species, taken as prey in England. Europeans obviously have far more patience for gathering data of this sort than do busy and dollar-obsessed Americans!

Now that we live in the city we rarely see *Mellinus*, despite a superabundance of dog droppings and their attendant flies. It is just as well that the wasps do not occur here commonly. If we were to lie prone on a city sidewalk peering at dog droppings we would doubtless end up in the nearest asylum.

13

Clark's Nutcrackers

ON AUTUMN DAYS we often heard harsh calls from the tops of nearby pine trees, to be answered by equally harsh calls from more distant trees. These were Clark's nutcrackers that had descended from their usual haunts higher in the mountains, close to timberline. What the messages were that they conveyed to one another from treetops, we had no idea, nor do we know why they appear to prefer lower altitudes for a few months each fall. These birds are reported to live mostly on a diet of pine seeds, which they whack from the cones with their powerful beaks. Perhaps they find seeds more plentiful at this season on our ponderosa pines than on the whitebark and limber pines where they usually live. However, we have never seen them harvesting pine seeds in our neighborhood. The seeds of ponderosa pines are known to be less nutritious than those of the pines on which the birds usually feed. Production of cones varies a good deal from year to year. Perhaps the nutcrackers that invaded our air space were scouting for good sources of cones, whatever the species.

As they flew from tree to tree the birds displayed colors reminding us of the cold places where they usually live. The light gray bodies are like worn snow, but there are patches of pure white on the black wings and on the sides of the black tail. They fly with deep, slow wingbeats in an undulating pattern, rather like woodpeckers. Not surprisingly, William Clark called them woodpeckers when he first spotted them in Idaho on the famous expedition of 1804–1806. Individuals he collected found their way to pioneer ornithologist Alexander Wilson, who called the species "Clark's crow," a suitable name since these are members of the crow family. Clark's nutcrackers have a limited range, from southwestern Canada to the mountains of California, Arizona, and New Mexico, always in mountainous country. We felt honored that they now and then appeared in our neighborhood, even though they had nothing to say but hoarse "kraaks" from treetops. They disdained our feeders, though we were generous with sunflower seeds that were surely as nutritious as pine seeds.

Clark's nutcrackers are known to breed as early as March, a time of bitter weather in the high country. Females have been seen incubating eggs in snowstorms, with the temperature close to zero. For most birds mere survival would be problematic at that season, and there would be little if any proteinaceous food available for nestlings. But pine seeds are rich in protein, and nutcrackers need only to macerate the seeds to feed their young. Pine seeds mature in late summer and are in short supply through the winter and spring, but nutcrackers have solved that dilemma. They are food hoarders *par excellence*. When the seeds are ripe, the birds whack the cones apart with their bills, then collect them in a pouch beneath their tongues. These pouches are quite expandable, and may contain many seeds, sometimes as many as a hundred at a time. Seed-laden birds then fly to caching sites, usually on cliff sides or south-facing slopes that are somewhat wind-swept of snow. Here they bury the seeds an inch or two deep in the soil in groups of up to ten. When finished, the birds rake soil or litter over the site with their bills, sometimes adding a stick or a cone. Several caches may be made in the same area, and several nutcrackers may share the same hillside, but not individual caches. Seed-laden birds may fly several miles from the point where the seeds were harvested to suitable caching sites.

Researchers have found that a single nutcracker may store from twenty thousand to a hundred thousand seeds. Since each cache contains only a few seeds, each bird must remember several thousand hiding places. It is estimated that it takes about ten thousand seeds to support a nut-cracker from October to April, and of course more if it is feeding young. Diana Tomback, working in the Sierras of California in the 1970s, found that the average nutcracker makes about seventy seven hundred caches of whitebark pine seeds. These would provide three times the nutritional requirements of an adult bird. Clearly more seeds are buried than are needed, compensating for losses to rodents and for failures to find cached seeds. Diana Tomback made several artificial caches and found that over ninety percent of the seeds were taken by rodents. Rodents may use smell to locate caches (but there is no evidence that nutcrackers do, birds having a notoriously poor sense of smell). Under natural conditions, loss to rodents is far less than this, since cliff sides and south-facing slopes are not sites where rodents usually flourish.

When retrieving seeds, the birds dig with side-sweeping motions of the bill, then pick up the seeds and store them in their pouches. When necessary, they may dig through several inches of snow that have covered the caching area. When the young have left the nest, they may accompany their parents to the caches and be fed there.

The ability of nutcrackers to remember accurately the location of so many caches, after several weeks and at some distance from sites of harvest and from nests, has long amazed biologists. Clearly they memorize major landmarks as well as smaller details of the terrain. Alan Kamil and his colleagues at the University of Nebraska captured several Clark's nutcrackers and kept them in an observation room, where they were fed pine seeds at the halfway point between a yellow and a green object. They quickly learned to find the seeds even when the distance between the landmarks was varied. Evidently the birds had learned the relationship between the landmarks. Such an ability to appreciate geometric patterns is unusual, but no doubt essential to the birds. These are hardly "bird-brained" creatures, as we usually describe members of the avian world (and people too, sometimes).

Clark's nutcrackers find a high percentage of their caches, even though they leave no specific cues to mark their cache sites. One investigator raked and smoothed over the soil where there were caches, yet the birds found the caches readily. Another researcher rearranged soil features in one half of an experimental enclosure, but not on the other half. The birds were about equally successful in finding caches on the two sides. We were greatly impressed to learn of the ability of these birds, since we, with our very much larger brains, often cannot even remember where we left our glasses.

Along Trail Ridge Road, in Rocky Mountain National Park, Clark's nutcrackers will sometimes accept snacks from tourists. In spring, the birds add insects to the macerated pine seeds they feed to nestlings, and caged birds will cache bits of mammalian flesh. However, they do not visit road kills in the manner of their relatives, the ravens and magpies. Their preferred food is the nut-like seeds of the whitebark pine, and it is believed that nutcrackers have been important in the dispersal of these high-altitude trees. Seeds that have been cached but not harvested often germinate, producing new stands of whitebark pines. The birds may also have played a role in the dispersal of other kinds of pines.

Although many aspects of the caching behavior of nut-crackers are unique, there are many other birds that cache food during periods of abundance and harvest it when food is scarce. Acorn woodpeckers of the southwestern states make holes in the bark of trees in which to store acorns, and shrikes impale insects and small birds on thorns or barbed wire until they are needed as food. Owls of many kinds store prey in larders near the nest; snowy owls have been seen to pile lemmings around their nest when these rodents are plentiful. In his book *Food Hoarding in Animals*, Stephen B. Vander Wall cites many instances of food storage, not only in birds but in mammals such as squirrels, marmots, and pikas. Food storage by woodrats we have discussed in another chapter. Many of these animals could not survive without laying in food for lean times.

Some insects, too, store food to carry them through periods when no food is available. Honeybees would never survive our winters were they not able to store quantities of honey following the nectar flows of summer. Harvester ants (those of the classic tale of the grasshopper and the ant) collect seeds through the summer and store them deep in the soil through the winter. Some nests contain more than a pound of grass and weed seeds. The nests of honey ants contain "repletes," individual worker ants that are used as "honey barrels." They accept nectar and honeydew from other workers to the point that their abdomens swell balloon-like. They then regurgitate honey whenever needed by colony members. Australian aborigines sometimes dug out the nests of honey ants and popped the swollen abdomens of the repletes into their mouths, rather like lollypops.

In all these cases long-term storage serves to carry the animals through periods when less food is available. But there are examples of short-term caching that serve other functions. Mountain lions and other large predators often cover their prey with soil, sticks, or snow, then return later to feed further. In this way they protect their prey from scavengers and help retard spoilage, while they wait until they are hungry again.

A very temporary kind of food caching occurs in some wasps, such as the caterpillar-hunters we discussed in another chapter. In this case the prey is placed in a clump of grass or the crotch of a plant while the wasp digs a nest nearby. In this way the prey is protected, at least to some degree, from marauding ants or other predators or scavengers.

The Clark's nutcrackers that reappeared each year in our neighborhood flourished because they had evolved behavior that permitted them to exploit a food source not usually sought by other birds, and to do so by harvesting seeds when abundant and using them as needed. Other animals cache food in other ways and so solve similar or different problems of survival. Each species is unique in its own way, and every one has stories to tell if we are not too preoccupied with our own technology to stop and inquire.

14

Pollen Wasps

FOR THOSE WITH a sense of beauty and the ability to resist the relentless rush of modern life, there are, each season, wildflowers glittering from every meadow, every streamside, every rocky outcrop. The drama begins with spring beauties (Claytonia), diminutive but most welcome harbingers of spring. We used to seek them on south-facing slopes, beside rocks that have been warmed by the sun, sometimes as early as late February, more often in March or April. Pasque flowers soon follow, springing up in unexpected places and luring early bees to their azure blossoms. Others follow in season, until at last a few lingering purple asters are left by the roadside before very different flowers are etched on the windows by frost.

Plants have personalities that are as marked as those of animals, if one is alert to them. I speak of the individuality of species, each with its own preferences for soil type and moisture levels, its survival mechanisms vis-à-vis herbivores, its ability to attract pollinators and seed dispersers. One might perhaps extend this to individual plants, which of course in nature differ according to both genetics and precise environment. However, I would hesitate to analyze the personality of each plant in a cornfield or the grasses in a suburban lawn. Generally we accept plants and animals as members of a species, whether it is a rabbit, a robin, or a rose.

That people take pleasure in the colors and odors of flowers is, in a way, remarkable, for of course flowers have evolved to serve very different functions than to brighten our walks or decorate funeral parlors. When Linnaeus, back in the mid-eighteenth century, proposed classifying plants according to their sexual organs, the pistils and stamens and the surrounding petals that lure pollinators, it was a shock to the sensibilities of many persons. Samuel Goodenough, Bishop of Carlisle, spoke of the "gross prurience of Linnaeus' mind," and even Goethe feared that women and young people would be embarrassed by botanical textbooks that discussed "the dogma of sexuality."

The variety of floral structures is astounding, all the way from the simple blossoms of buttercups to the complex ones of orchids, and the odors they produce vary from the ultimate in fragrance to the most repellent, rather like feces or carrion. Foul-smelling blossoms are, however, as attractive to beetles and flies as are the most fragrant to bees and butterflies.

Pollen wasps are specialists in exploiting relatively complex blossoms, in our area chiefly penstemon (beardtongue) and phacelia (scorpion weed). The largest of our local species is a specialist on one-sided penstemon (*Penstemon unilateralis*), while two smaller species are specialists on species of *Phacelia*. These are both plants with relatively complex, bluish blossoms, though they belong to different families of plants. The pollen wasps are, however, closely related, all belonging to the genus *Pseudomasaris* in the family Vespidae (a family that also includes yellow jackets, potter wasps, and other kinds that are flesh-feeders). It is surely odd that pollen wasps have departed from the usual food-preferences of their group and assumed bee-like behavior. It is especially odd that they have come to specialize on a just a few unrelated plants among the many that bloom in the same season and in similar places. It would be more easily explained if penstemon and phacelia were not visited by bees, leaving that niche empty for pollen wasps to fill. But that is not the case; pollen wasps compete with bumblebees and other kinds of bees for the nectar and pollen in the blossoms.

In other parts of the world there are other kinds of pollen wasps, all belonging to a discrete group that evolved from predatory wasps. These wasps are bee-like in their behavior but not in structure. Their bodies are not especially hairy, and they have no "pollen baskets" or other devices for carrying pollen to the nest. Rather, they ingest pollen and nectar and carry the mixture in their crops, then regurgitate it into the nest cells. These are not social insects, like yellow jackets or bumblebees; each female has her own, independent nest.

We sometimes used to find the nests of pollen wasps glued to rocks near our home. Each is made up of several cylindrical earthen cells, attached side by side. They are often built in exposed places, but they are not easy to spot, being colored much the same as the rocks that bear them. Nor are they easy to open, requiring a hammer or another rock to break through the tough outer covering. Sometimes nest remnants persist for several years after they have been abandoned by the wasps. These tough-walled nests contrast with those of typical mud daubers and mason wasps, which use a mixture of soil and water. Pollen wasps mix soil and nectar, perhaps with some salivary fluids, and produce a mortar that is very hard indeed.

One-sided penstemon is our tallest and most showy penstemon. During some summers the meadows below our house were blue with the tall wands of these plants, while in other summers there were few. Most of the tubular, inch-long blossoms are on one side of the stem, hence the name "one-sided." The many flowers on the stalk bloom in sequence, from bottom to top, so that for several weeks there are always some in bloom.

Female pollen wasps ascend the stalks spirally (on the wing) and attack the blossoms vigorously, ramming their bodies into the slender tubes repeatedly. By so doing they gain access to the nectar deep in the blossoms while scraping their backs over the anthers that bear the pollen. The wasps later scrape pollen from their backs by preening movements of the front legs, then swallow it, later to be regurgitated into the nest. Both males and females take nectar to fuel themselves, but only females take pollen to the nests.

Penstemon blossoms are uniquely designed to accommodate pollen wasps and long-tongued bees, while providing no rewards for short-tongued bees and other insects. One of the stamens is so designed that the wasp must jerk its body downwards and backwards and so gain access to the nectar while rubbing its back over the pollen-bearing anthers.

One of my former students, Robert Longair, studied these wasps for three summers in Hewlett Gulch, a few miles downstream on the creek that flowed through the meadow below our house. In July the gulch is filled with flowers, including stands of one-sided penstemon that are visited by pollen wasps. They spend only a few seconds at a blossom before going on to another. Clumps of plants are also visited by males, and Rob was interested in determining whether males defend individual plants or clumps from other males. After marking males with paint spots, he found that some males do remain within or near a clump of plants for some time, perching or flying off to investigate insects that enter the patch. Other males patrol between patches, and some alternate between the two behaviors. Once in a while males chase one another, and occasionally they face off in the air and may strike one another. Rarely, they grapple and may fall to the ground before separating.

Males approach females when they are in flight or on a flower, then grasp them from behind and begin to stroke the sides of the females' heads with their antennae. The males' antennae have a terminal, concave club that they place over the sides of the females' heads. With a series of strokes of the fully extended antennae, the male moves slightly farther back with each stroke and soon extends his genitalia. Mating is accompanied by a loud buzzing and the pair may fall to the ground before separating. One male was seen to mate six times, but most mated only once during Rob's periods of observation. Females were often harassed by males during their foraging, and time spent on flowers was greatly reduced when males were present. Although males vary somewhat in size, there was no evidence that larger males are more successful in defending a territory or in mating more frequently.

This method of bringing the sexes together works well for this species of pollen wasp, since females visit only one kind of plant that grows in clumps that can easily be located. Other species exploit plants that are much more widely dispersed. John Alcock, of Arizona State University, studied a species in which females visit plants that are scarce and widely dispersed through the desert. Here males perch on rocks in open areas on hilltops, which serve as landmarks that are visited by females. In one South African species, the nests of the females are aggregated, so that it is advantageous for males to seek females at their nests. In still another South African species, females visit pools to collect water for making their mud nests, and mating occurs at the pools. South Africa has many species of pollen wasps, and it is a South African, Sarah Gess, who has written the definitive book, *Pollen Wasps*, published in 1996 by Harvard

University Press. In pollen wasps, as in many kinds of wasps and bees, males have evolved a variety of searching strategies that are effective in leading them to females.

The pollen wasps that lived near our mountain home were handsome animals, brightly patterned with yellow but unique because of the long, clubbed antennae of the males. Most persons might be content to call them yellow jackets, and although they may share a remote common ancestry with yellow jackets, they have evolve a wholly different life style, evident only upon careful observation. We were fortunate to have them as neighbors.

15

Crossbills

WE HAD NEVER before lived in an environment dominated by conifers. It was exciting to become intimately acquainted not only with ponderosa pines and Douglas-firs, but with creatures closely associated with them: pine and tassel-eared squirrels, Clark's nutcrackers, pine siskins, and those most eccentric of birds, red crossbills. Crossbills were almost always with us, chattering in small groups from trees or flying past uttering their distinctive "chip-chip" calls. Now and then they came to our feeders, sampling a diet different from their usual one of pine seeds. Crossbills are finches in which the upper and lower mandibles of the beak are curved and drawn out to sharp points, the upper mandible slightly longer and crossing over the lower. With these instruments, crossbills are expert at extracting seeds from the cones of conifers before they are fully open. The beak is inserted between the overlapping scales, then widened by opening the mandibles slightly; the seed is then lifted out and husked with the help of the palate.

Legend has it that the birds twisted their beaks when trying to pull the nails from the cross, permitting themselves to be smeared with the blood of Jesus. Their red is not that of blood, really, but rather a dull, neutral red, somewhat brighter on the rump. Only the mature males are of this color. The females and immatures are olive-gray, though young males may also have streaks and patches of red.

The origin of the beak, so different from that of other birds, has been a matter of discussion among biologists for many years. It puzzled Charles Darwin, who believed that evolution by natural selection "must advance by the shortest and slowest steps." How to account for so novel a structure, unless Darwin was wrong and the unusual beaks appeared suddenly, producing a "hopeful monster" in one step? It proved useful to compare the twenty-five species and subspecies of crossbills, which vary a good deal in body size as well as in bill size and dimensions, depending upon the kinds of cones available within their range. The white-winged crossbills of the Far North feed mostly on soft cones such as those of larches and spruces, and their bills are somewhat more slender than those of red crossbills. Various races of red crossbills also show variation in bill dimensions, depending upon the conifers abundant within their habitat. So the robust beaks of our local crossbills, which are adapted for twisting apart the scales of the large, tough cones of ponderosa pines, no doubt evolved from bills that were less robust.

Craig Benkman, of New Mexico State University, found that red crossbills prefer trees that produce cones regularly and hold them through the winter, but races have developed that exploit different "key conifers" by evolving a slightly different size of beak and palate. The smallest race, with the least powerful beak, lives in coastal forests of western hemlock. Hemlock cones are small and do not require the heavy equipment of birds that exploit ponderosa pines. Races favoring Douglas-fir forests have beaks and palates of intermediate size, reflecting the use of cones of intermediate size and hardness. He found that individuals of each race were able to obtain seeds most rapidly when attacking cones for which they were best adapted. All were able to take the seeds from closed cones effectively, in contrast to pine siskins, which lack crossed bills and can only take seeds from open cones.

Craig Benkman and his colleague Anna Lindholm performed some clever experiments that are further suggestive concerning the evolution of crossbill's beaks. Using seven captive red crossbills, they clipped off the tips of the beaks of four of them with nail clippers, such that they no longer crossed, leaving the other three birds as controls. The clipped birds suffered no ill effects, as there are no nerve endings in the beaks; it was an operation similar to people trimming their fingernails. The four did well extracting seeds from open cones, but were unable to open closed cones. As the beaks slowly grew longer and resumed their crossing, the birds gradually improved their performance, and when the beaks were 90 percent of their original length they were able to open cones as well as the controls. Benkman and Lindholm suggested that crossbills may have evolved from a bird rather like a siskin, and that any slight twisting of the beak proved advantageous and was enhanced by natural selection as generations followed one another. Nestlings, incidentally, have uncrossed beaks, and the lengthening and crossing of the mandibles develops gradually, much as they may have developed during evolution. Once having developed their unique bills, crossbills were able to exploit a source of food unavailable to other birds. No doubt their main competitors for conifer seeds are squirrels, but squirrels feed on other things as well. Squirrels must make-do with what they can find locally, since they lack the ability to seek food over wide areas, as crossbills do.

At our feeders, it was easy to contrast the curious beaks of crossbills with those of pine siskins and Cassin's finches, which are more generalized feeders. By having become specialists on pine seeds, crossbills have placed themselves at a major disadvantage. Cone crops vary greatly from place to place and time to time; the birds must explore areas where conifers are plentiful and must be constantly in search of seed-bearing cones. They have become wanderers.

Ludlow Griscom, who published a detailed study of these birds in 1937, wrote that "the red crossbill is a bird of curious contradictions. Possessed of remarkably vagrant and erratic habits ... it is apparently indifferent to temperature, humidity, and altitude." Red crossbills range throughout much of North America and Eurasia, even parts of North Africa and India, wherever there are suitable coniferous forests. Always they travel in groups. When a flock arrives in a grove of conifers, individuals set about to pick at the cones. Flock members observe one another, in this way sharing information so that the group need spend little time there if not much food is available. Flock members also warn one another if a predator (such as a goshawk) is close by. So there are real advantages in traveling in flocks rather than as solitary individuals. Flock size varies from just a few to well over a hundred. Splitting and combining of flocks probably is frequent, depending upon food availability. The flocks that we saw around our house varied from six to twenty, though once on a hike we saw a flock of at least fifty. Watching them, one gets the impression that the birds spend so much time seeking food that they can't take time to mate and build nests. But of course they do.

This brings us to another peculiarity of crossbills. Unlike most birds, they show little response to day length and so usually do not nest in early summer to take advantage of the abundance of insects. Their major response is to the abundance of pine seeds. So they may breed at any time of year, whenever there is plentiful food for them. Nesting in January through April is common, but nests have been found in other months, in fact in every month of the year. Fall brings a new crop of mature cones that persist through the winter and into early spring. Summer presents the birds with immature cones and old, open cones of the previous crop. So summer may be somewhat stressful for crossbills. They do sometimes take insects, but they are evidently able to rear their young successfully on macerated pine seeds.

Nests are not easy to find, as they are built fairly high in evergreen trees. We have never seen a nest and have no evidence that they nested anywhere near our home. Nests are reported to be built of twigs, with a lining of grasses and feathers, and three or four eggs are laid there. Since nesting often occurs in cold weather, the female may have to brood persistently for several weeks while she is fed by the male.

We humans have a hankering for seeing unusual creatures, so we visit zoos, take African safaris, and invent weird, extraterrestrial monsters. And all the while some of the oddest of birds are here at hand, quietly extracting and husking pine seeds over our heads and flashing red among the branches.

16

Beewolves and
Other Quests

OUR SMALL HOUSE was so situated that wildlife seemed
to accept it as part of the landscape, and through our windows we could participate vicariously in a good many natural events. But there were many times when we were lured
out-of-doors in a quest for information or for aesthetic
rewards. After a fresh snow in winter, there were animal
tracks to be examined, and snowdrifts to be studied for the
presence of wingless scorpion flies. In April and May it was
time to follow queen bumblebees and see if they had yet
established nests. Already thatcher ants would be busy on
their mounds, as we wrote about in an earlier chapter. In
June it was worth checking bushes along a nearby creek to
listen for yellowthroats, and a tangle of hawthorns to learn
if our yellow-breasted chat had returned. Deer fawns
would be hiding in the grass, and meadow arnicas splashing
orange-yellow across damp meadows. By midsummer it
was hard to find excuses to stay *indoors*, and like as not we
would eat lunch on some convenient hillside and sleep at
night on our deck, or farther afield.

It was worth a hike or two to a nearby valley to check the
beaver dams, and perhaps to bring back a trout. This was
the only place we knew of where spotted saxifrage grew,

delicate, moss-like plants with pale blossoms dotted with purple. Here, too, grew lavender kitten-tails (*Besseya*, named for a prominent botanist). Where the stream entered the forest, there were blue columbines in abundance, Colorado's state flower. With luck we might see a dipper (or water ouzel) diving into the stream in search of mayfly nymphs.

There were frequent trips in late June or early July to a hill about five miles away where several events required attention. Here was located one of the swarms of dance flies we wrote about in an earlier chapter, and here was the horizontal limb of a pine favored by a male blue grouse for his annual performance. But our major objective was the study of the male beewolves that had assumed possession of small plots of ground among the rocky outcrops and scattered pine trees. They were totally reliable, and appeared during the last week in June for every one of the thirteen years we lived in the mountains. Beewolves are small wasps of the genus *Philanthus*. The name is Greek for flower-lover; beewolves visit flowers for nectar, and the females capture bees there, usually small sweat bees. The bees are paralyzed by stinging and carried to a nest deep in the soil, where they serve as food for the larvae.

Beewolves have been popular objects of research for many years, beginning as early as 1799, when French entomologist P.A. Latreille found the wasps nesting along a road near Paris. They were favorites of pioneer naturalist Jean-Henri Fabre toward the end of the nineteenth century, as they were of mid-twentieth century animal behaviorist Niko Tinbergen. We have included chapters about them in two books, and (with Kevin M. O'Neill) have devoted a whole book covering (at least briefly) the natural history of twenty-four of the thirty-four North American species. So why bother to study them further? In part because we were intrigued by the fact that males in this population reappeared each year in exactly the same places occupied by males the previous year. It is easy to understand how wrens return to the same nest box each year, and hummingbirds to the same patch of flowers. Birds have good memories for resources important to them. But beewolves, like most insects, live no more than a year, and as winged adults for only a few weeks. A beewolf cannot remember the site occupied by an individual of the previous generation he has never met. Nor is it likely that he is responding to a chemical cue left there by last year's wasps, since the site has been subject to months of rain and snow, and the vegetation differs in details each year. It is a tantalizing problem.

First, a few more details. The species here is *Philanthus crabroniformis*, a ponderous name for an attractive black and yellow wasp (*crabroniformis* might be translated "rather like a wasp," which is redundant if not a bit silly). We'll call the species "Crab" for short. Female beewolves dig their nests in places more or less bare of vegetation and where the soil is easy to dig in. In our area, there were few such sites, principally along road cuts or on eroded slopes. We had trouble finding nests and the few we found were widely scattered.

The males would have had difficulty finding females under such conditions, and they had formed a "lek" near the top of this hill comparable to the leks of grouse, where males gather, perform their rituals, and attract females from afar. In another chapter, we mentioned hilltopping in butterflies, a similar gathering place for sexual encounters. Other species of beewolves have been known to form leks, so that in itself was not a surprise. However, a population of Crab we had studied in Wyoming behaved differently. Here there was ample space for nests along sandy trails, and at least fifteen females had formed a nesting aggregation.

About an equal number of males had established territories about a hundred fifty feet upwind of the nests.

We must explain that each male occupies a territory on the ground two or three feet in diameter. Here he assumes a central perch and flies off periodically to scent-mark surrounding grasses and other vegetation. There are scent glands in the male's head, and brushes on both the head and the abdomen that serve to spread the scent (called a pheromone). Each territory is defended from other males and other flying insects by aggressive flights. When a female, attracted by the scent, flies by, the male is quick to follow her and the pair mate on the ground (all very reminiscent of the bumblebees we discussed in an earlier chapter). It is easy to see why, in the Wyoming population, the males had established themselves upwind of the nests, as the pheromone would be carried to the females. Although the pheromones are highly volatile, they cannot be detected by the inefficient noses of people.

In the population near our home, males had established their territories far from any known nests, in an area about fifteen by thirty yards, just downwind from the top of the hill. It seemed likely that the combined pheromone of the males might drift over a considerable area. There were, in various years, from seven to twenty territorial males comprising the lek. Not only did the same patch of hillside attract males each year, but each male occupied the precise territorial space that had been occupied the previous year. We recognized two "prime territories," occupied every day of the active period every year, and others that were often occupied but not every day or every year. We marked each male with a paint spot and found that, each year, the same males would return each day to the same territory (after spending the night elsewhere). Each territorial space was no more than a bare place surrounded by small plants; other places that looked similar to us were not accepted. What cues did the males use in locating exactly the same spots each year? One of the prime territories was eventually abandoned after the site became heavily shaded and covered with pine needles. That suggests a partial answer: the spot must be sunny at least much of the day, and it must be more or less bare in the center. Elsewhere (working on a different species) we were able to create artificial territorial spaces that were sometimes occupied by wasps.

One year we removed twelve males from their territories and placed them in fixative so they could be submitted to biochemists for analysis of the pheromones. Each territory was reoccupied by another male within four to forty-three minutes. One other territory was reoccupied four times within twenty minutes as successive males were removed. Obviously there were other males around waiting to take over superior spaces, and there was something special about these spaces.

That, in a nutshell, was the extent of our observations on the hillside. But there was a deep, V-shaped valley about half a mile away where, along the sides of the gulley at the bottom, males of another species had formed a lek. This species was *Philanthus barbatus* (*barbatus* is Latin for "bearded," a reference to the hair brushes used to apply pheromone). We'll call the species "Barb" for short. Barb and Crab are very similar and are closely related species, but the yellow bands on Crab are replaced by white in Barb. Females of both species have widely scattered nests and males of both had established leks evidently serving to attract females from a wide area. Barb appeared in the field a few weeks later than Crab, and our trips to the valley took place in August and early September.

Male territories of Barb were scattered along the sides of the gulley, in bare spots among tall grasses, and most scent-marking was on these grasses. Here there were also two prime territories, occupied each day we checked the site, each year, and there were a dozen or so others that were occupied off and on. Once again we collected several for pheromone analysis, and within a short time the same spaces were occupied by other males. So clearly there were other males around, ready to occupy spots from which they had previously been barred by aggression from the first occupants. Once again we had studied the species elsewhere and found aggregated nests, with male territories not far away.

The pheromones were identified by biochemist friends and found to be complex and each species quite different chemically. The leks of the two species were only half a mile apart and in most years there was a week or two when the active periods overlapped. So it would be important that the widely dispersed females recognized the pheromone of their own species. Why males of one species, in our area, aggregated near the top of a hill and those of another did so at the bottom of a deep valley is a mystery. Both are prominent landmarks and doubtless a landmark of some sort was important for the wasps to orient to; but why the difference?

There are other mysteries. How does a male, freshly emerged from a nest made last year, "decide" whether to join a lek remote from his natal nest or (as is true in other populations) set up a territory near the nests of last year? Does he evaluate the distribution of females busy at digging nests? (It seems to us unlikely that there are genetic differences between lek-formers and non-lek-formers, but this hasn't been studied). How does a male find precisely the same territorial spot occupied by a male of the previous season? Does he fly about and evaluate the available spaces? All of this seems to require more judgment than we commonly attribute to insects. But "judgment" need not involve the careful weighing of alternatives the way we do. Inherited behavior patterns are not completely inflexible but allow for alternative modes of performance depending upon sensory input from the environment. So males may indeed have options, though how they are exercised in this case we really cannot visualize. Does a male inherit a "blueprint" of a desirable lekking area and a suitable territorial space, a blueprint that includes a particular arrangement of trees, grasses, shrubs, bare patches of soil, and so forth?

We often spent hours watching an individual territory, and it was hard not to put thoughts into the heads of male beewolves. Shall I mark this stem or that? Here is an intruder; shall I attack? Shall I pursue this passing butterfly, or wait patiently for a female beewolf? Of course a wasp, or any other insect, lacks the ability to think such thoughts (or at least we assume so). But one cannot help wondering how they manage to do so well at survival with such minuscule brains. Long term survival may be more certain for small-brained creatures that usually make the right decisions, even though they lack the ability to think about the pros and cons as we do. Human culture, for all its wonderful manifestations, fills us with mindsets that can lead to decisions that can sometimes be deadly.

17

The Trail

AVERAGE ANNUAL PRECIPITATION at our mountain home was approximately fifteen inches. By any definition, we lived in a semidesert. South-facing slopes were largely bare of trees and covered with dry-adapted grasses, prickly pear cacti, yuccas, and occasionally small junipers. North-facing slopes were generally forested with Douglas-firs, which rarely reached a height of more than fifty feet. Flatter ground, or east- or west-facing slopes, favored well-spaced ponderosa pines, handsome, spreading trees but not really "ponderous" like those of the Pacific Northwest, where David Douglas discovered the trees in 1820. In such a setting, even the most evanescent of springs and streamlets provided welcome plant diversity.

We had not lived long on our granite cliff before we discovered the pleasures of hiking in nearby canyons. Even the smallest were habitat for wildflowers, birds, and insects not seen elsewhere. We built a trail down the nearest of these, not only for ourselves but marked so that others might enjoy it. We hiked it so often that every detail sticks in our memories. The stream was minuscule, and during most summers its lower reaches were dry. It began as a permanent spring and descended perhaps five hundred feet before reaching a meadow below, with many a minor waterfall and an occasional small pool where water striders held forth.

We sometimes hiked it in winter, when we had to plow through the deep snow that had collected there. Even so, the walls of the canyon to some degree protected us from the howling winds. There were usually a few Steller's jays and mountain chickadees about, and ravens cruising overhead. On a day in March, when much of the snow had gone, we found pale green catkins dangling from the alders, and "pussies" on some of the willows and aspens. Spring beauties (*Claytonia*) bloomed along the trail, the first flowers of spring. Only a few other green plants began to show, and we turned our attention to the mosses and lichens, ever dependable. We have always felt that to fully appreciate nature, one should be able to name the plants and animals. We confess that we knew the names of hardly any of the mosses and lichens, but an early spring hike would be less rewarding without them.

But most of our memories are of the warmer months of the year. Near the beginning of the trail there were damp places, shaded by alders and willows. Giant angelicas grew here, hollow-stemmed plants of the parsnip family growing head-high, plants with many uses in folk medicine. Close to the ground there were blue violets and pink water spring beauties (*Montia*). Soon the trail entered a stand of tall narrow-leaved cottonwoods and ponderosa pines, the haunt of pine squirrels that usually announced their annoyance at being disturbed by angry chattering. Once we met a young black bear there, but he absconded quickly.

By a bend in the trail, each year, coral-root orchids grew in clumps, each clump no doubt arising from a mass of rich loam. These are saprophytes, living on decaying organic matter, but orchids none the less, with all the usual delicate floral parts. The roots are said to resemble coral, but we have never disturbed the plants to confirm this.

A slope a bit farther along was partially covered with kinnikinnik, the Indian name for a plant that occurs throughout

the Northern Hemisphere, usually called bearberry elsewhere. The wonderful scientific name is *Arctostaphylos uva-
ursi*, which means bearberry in both Greek and Latin. Evidently the Swedish naturalist Carl Linnaeus, who named the
plant, knew something about the feeding habits of bears.
Indians and early settlers shared the berries with bears and
other animals, though they are pulpy and must be cooked
and sweetened to make them palatable as food for people.
The evergreen leaves can be dried and smoked, and are said
to have a slightly narcotic effect. We found the sight of these
low, spreading plants, whether in the spring with their bell-
shaped flowers, or later with their red berries, to be sufficient, without recourse to narcosis or gormandizing.

Elsewhere on the slope there were pasque flowers in
spring, and over the next few weeks larkspur and scarlet
globeflower. All three are members of the buttercup family
and therefore poisonous if people or their livestock were to
eat them—not that this diminishes their beauty in any way.
Further on, the trail enters a more densely wooded area,
with alders, river birches, and a tangle of wild raspberries
close to the stream on the left, Rocky Mountain maples,
serviceberries, and pines on the right. In June we were welcomed to this glade by MacGillivray's warblers—rich and
vibrant songs for such small birds. Often a search for them
was in vain, as the birds preferred to remain deep in the
bushes. Audubon named the birds for William Mac-
Gillivray, who helped him immeasurably while he was writing his *Ornithological Biography*.

Of course there were other bird songs. On a good day we
might hear black-headed grosbeaks, solitary and warbling
vireos, cordilleran flycatchers, and on an especially good day
an olive-sided flycatcher calling "quick more beer" from a
treetop. During one spring several veeries passed through,
each practicing his ethereal scale-descending phrases. We

think of veeries as eastern birds, but they do nest in the mountains of Colorado, and we had been lucky enough to find them on their way to the high country.

In shady places, in June, there were stands of false Solomon's seal, bearing waxy green leaves and a small group of star-shaped white flowers. They are called "false" from a resemblance to "true" Solomon's seal, but who decided which is true and which is false we do not know. Wild lily-of-the-valley is a better name. On a sunny hillside, Sego lilies bloomed, their complex, cup-shaped blossoms defying ready description. In his book *Edible Native Plants of the Rocky Mountains*, H.D. Harrington lists both these members of the lily family as having edible roots that were sometimes consumed by Indians and early settlers. Even a hungry person must have paused before digging up such lovely plants.

In a very special place, the stream flowed thinly over flat, mossy rocks, and here grew shooting-stars each June, some years a great many, some years just a few. Shooting-stars are primroses in which the pink petals turn upward, the dark stamens forming a tube facing downward, as if the flowers were about to shoot to the ground. They stand on stems eight to fifteen inches tall, well above the basal leaves. It is a display, we like to think, reserved only for ardent nature-lovers like ourselves.

The sides of the canyon, part way down, become more precipitous, and on one side there is a cliff perhaps seventy feet high. The granitic rocks have an abundance of ledges and crevices, where animals had lived, for below some of them there are vertical streaks of orange lichens, where someone (perhaps a woodrat) had found a convenient place to urinate regularly. Elsewhere the rocks are gray to pink-ish, depending upon their feldspar content, and covered with dark greenish lichens, with a *Jamesia* bush here and there. The cliff forms a background for a grove of tall aspens, their leaves in season pale green, rich green, or golden, always quaking in whatever breeze they can catch.

The trail here was bordered with ninebark (*Physocarpos*), a member of the rose family bearing abundant clusters of white, sweet-smelling blossoms that attracted many bees and butterflies. The bark of these shrubs is continually shredding, revealing new layers of bark, as if it had "nine lives." A bit further on, yellow puccoons (*Lithospermum*) bloomed in midsummer. Puccoon is an Indian word for these plants, useful for the yellow pigments they yielded.

One year there was a partially consumed mule deer carcass beside the trail. Had it been the prey of a mountain lion, or had it been wounded by a hunter and later attacked or scavenged by coyotes? The following summer only bones and bits of skin and fur remained, and skin beetles were doing their best to dispose of that.

On the lower part of the trail snowberry bushes (*Symphoricarpos*) abounded. These are members of the honeysuckle family, their trumpet-shaped pink flowers attractive to bumblebees. In the fall, the flowers are replaced by white, pea-sized berries. We sometimes ate these, but found them relatively tasteless; perhaps birds enjoyed them more than we did. Red osier dogwood (*Cornus stolonifera*), a taller shrub that also grew here, has white fruits of similar size, but is most notable for its red bark. Indians are said to have shredded the bark, dried it, and smoked it. Here at the bottom of the canyon, pines and Douglas-firs reached unusual size, with massive trunks and tops towering perhaps a hundred feet above the trail.

The trail finally opened into the meadow below, a place where we used to harvest chokecherries and squaw currants. Here there were clumps of skunkbrush (*Rhus trilobata*), a plant related to poison ivy but non-poisonous and productive, in late summer, of attractive bunches of fuzzy, deep red berries. The bushes have a pleasant odor, not at all like that of skunks. The berries persist through the winter and provide a source of food when little else is available.

Vesper sparrows sang from the bushes in the meadow, lazuli buntings from trees along the stream. Red-tailed hawks soared on updrafts and snipe could sometimes be flushed from marshy places. In midsummer the meadow was multicolored, with blue penstemon, pink bergamot, and black-eyed susans, with tall yellow coneflowers in wet places. This is the meadow where we studied bumblebees, as described in another chapter.

The meadow is now posted and is becoming a housing development. That, of course, is how essays on environmental subjects usually end.

18

Marmots

RODENTS ARE COMMONLY considered the most lowly of animals: small, rather drably colored, and often up to no good. We had thirteen species at our mountain home, fourteen if we included the beavers that lived on a creek an easy hike away. Tassel-eared squirrels we thought quite beautiful and welcomed to our feeders. Woodrats, at the other extreme, annoyed us a good deal with their nocturnal activities under the house. We have already dedicated a chapter to each of these. Porcupines we met on one of the first days we visited our newly acquired property, when a big one rambled down a path through the woods. We never saw one again, though we often saw evidence of their damage to trees. The owner of one of the summer cabins in our area found that porcupines liked to gnaw on his house while he was away. Porcupines do not seem to like people, and people do not like them much either, especially if they have a dog that has tangled too closely with their formidable quills.

The most abundant of our rodent guests were the least chipmunks, the smallest of the five kinds of chipmunks that occur in Colorado. During the summer the chipmunks often drank from our birdbath, and in fall and spring they would sometimes climb up our window screens and jump off to the seed feeders. Now and then a chipmunk would produce a series of loud, rapid "chips" that might go on for several minutes, for no obvious reason unless trying to justify being called a chipmunk. Winters were spent in their burrows, living sleepily on food they had stored.

There were three kinds of ground squirrels. Golden-mantled ground squirrels were animals of the rocks, while Wyoming ground squirrels lived in burrows in nearby meadows. The third species, the rock squirrel, visited us only once, for a few days. Despite its bushy tail, this is classified as a ground squirrel, not a true (tree) squirrel like the pine and tassel-eared squirrels. There were the ubiquitous deer mice and voles, and plenty of pocket gophers, who left fresh piles of soil on local hillsides but stayed below ground most of the time. Sixty-four kinds of rodents are recorded in Colorado. We had less than a fourth of them, but we sometimes felt that we lived in a rather mousy world.

We have not so far mentioned the marmots, the largest of our rodents (aside from beavers), some of them weighing ten pounds or more. We found these lumbering animals attractive in their own way, with their brownish fur and short, bushy tail. The buffy cheeks and the white band across the face, just above the nose, gave them a somewhat aristocratic appearance. We seldom saw their undersides, which are dull yellowish in color, hence the name yellow-bellied marmot (*Marmota flaviventris*, which means just that in Latin). Often they are called rockchucks or whistle-pigs; easterners tend to call them woodchucks or groundhogs, though the eastern groundhog is a different and less interesting animal. Marmots prefer rocky terrain and range all the way from the foothills to well above timberline. We most often saw them sprawled out on top of the rocky outcrop adjacent to our deck, appearing to peer off to the distant peaks. No doubt they were simply sunning themselves, since it is doubtful that marmots have good distance vision, and rodents do not see colors.

Marmots lend themselves well to research on animal behavior, since they are large, diurnal, and easy to live-trap and mark with ear-tags or fur dyes. They live in small family groups, where individuals can easily be recognized and followed over time. Kenneth Armitage, of the University of Kansas, has spent much of his career studying marmots. We met him many years ago (we think it may have been 1964), when he was perched on a hilltop near the south gate of Yellowstone National Park recording the events in a local population of marmots. It was a splendid site, but to reach it one had to cross the Snake River, which had no bridge at that point, and the nearest biological station was some distance away. Subsequently, he shifted his research to the Rocky Mountain Biological Station, near Crested Butte, Colorado. Here, at an elevation of about ninety-five hundred feet, there are abundant marmots on patches of rocky outcrops in the flower-filled meadows. (Bill Calder, whom we met in the chapter on hummingbirds, worked in much the same area.) It proved a great place for a Kansan to spend the summer, as Armitage would admit. He and his students and associates made good use of their time and amassed a huge amount of data concerning these seemingly simple animals.

Marmots live in burrows that they dig, usually starting beneath rocks. The burrows remain the focus of their lives; they spend perhaps 80 percent of their lives there, more than half of that time in hibernation in the winter. Winters are very long at high altitudes, and they may remain in hibernation for seven or eight months, leaving only four or five in which to gorge themselves sufficiently to hibernate once again and in the meantime to mate and produce a new generation. When marmots first emerge, there may be snow still about and little greenery to serve as food. So they may have to rely on stored fat for a time. The time of snowmelt in their habitat is critically important. If snow lasts into midsummer, the females may not become robust enough to produce a litter, or the young may not grow large enough to survive the next winter.

Soon after they emerge, the males establish territories of an acre or two in extent in which there are several females. They defend their territories from other males and mate with the adult females. Over time yearling males that have overwintered in the burrows will be harassed until they leave, but yearling females may remain as part of the extended family. The number of females in the family varies from one to five, with an average of about 2.3. Males may retain much the same harem for several years, rarely as long as six years. According to Kenneth Armitage, the maximum male life span is about nine years, while females may live as long as fifteen years. Males are exposed to more predation as they seek out suitable territories. Young males may roam about a good deal after they leave the parental nest; some have been found as much as ten miles away. Fewer than a fourth of the young males are likely to reach reproductive age.

Within the burrow, young are born in early summer in a nest of grasses and other soft materials. The number of young per litter varies from three to eight, most commonly four. The young emerge from the den in July and feed and grow rapidly, reaching a size of four or five pounds before it is time to hibernate. Marmots feed on almost any kind of herbaceous plant growing nearby, flowers, fruit, and seeds as well as foliage, though they tend to avoid poisonous plants such as larkspur and lupine. We often saw tracks of cleared or matted vegetation leading from burrows. Since marmots move along slowly on their bellies and tend to use the same trails over and over, the trails are easy to spot.

On a typical day, marmots emerge at sun-up and graze for a time, then bask in the sun for a while before retreating to their burrows toward midday. In late afternoon they emerge to bask some more and feed some more before retiring for the night. As David Armstrong remarks in his book *Rocky Mountain Mammals,* "the program is that of tourists on well-earned vacations ... they eat or they sunbathe, and then they sleep." There is reason behind their laziness. After all, they do not have to go far or do much besides eating, and a sluggish animal can retain a low metabolic rate and let needed fat accumulate prior to a long winter of sleep.

Marmots are quiet animals most of the time. They never indulge in long episodes of chipping like chipmunks or angry chatter like disturbed pine squirrels. When closely related individuals meet one another they often nuzzle and expose their cheek glands to one another, or they may raise their tails and expose anal glands. When there is cause for alarm, for example when a coyote is spotted, the first individual to detect it emits a loud whistle (hence the name whistle-pig). Not only does the whistle alert other marmots, who run to their burrows, but at high altitudes pikas respond similarly, and at more moderate altitudes golden-mantled ground squirrels. Similarly, marmots respond to the alarm calls of pikas and golden-mantled ground squirrels. According to Walter Shriner, of the University of California at Davis, this is one of the very few instances of call recognition between different species of mammals other than primates. He found that both marmots and golden-mantled ground squirrels are able to distinguish alarm calls from other calls of either species as well as from other loud, non-threatening calls in the environment, such as birdcalls.

George Waring, of the University of Colorado, studied the meaning of marmot sounds by recording them and playing them back in the field. Besides the major alarm call, there are other whistles that denote mild alarm or aggression, as well as unmusical screams that are sometimes produced by a submissive individual being pursued by a dominant. Marmots that are simply annoyed may chatter their teeth. Evidently there is no "all clear" signal after a predator has left; the marmots simply resume feeding or basking. Alarm signals are evidently not used if an avian predator flies overhead.

Marmots often have an "escape burrow" to which they can retreat quickly if there is an alarm whistle. These are usually simpler than the two- or three-entrance burrows in which they breed and hibernate. Marmots grazing near a road often use dry culverts as escape burrows. Near our home, we found that marmots disturbed by the passage of a car would sometimes meet an early death as they crossed the road to the nearest culvert.

Coyotes are major predators of marmots as they are of other rodents and of rabbits. Badgers sometimes dig marmots from their burrows and weasels are slender enough to enter burrows and attack the young. Perhaps wolverines, wolves, and grizzly bears preyed upon marmots before they were driven to extinction throughout much of the Rockies. One of the advantages of group living is, of course, the presence of several pairs of eyes to spot a predator. Marmots are ever-vigilant and quick to sound the alarm.

There are other advantages in group living, such as the sharing of body heat when several individuals hibernate together. There are also disadvantages. Infanticide has occasionally been reported, but the reasons for it are not understood. Both males and females have been seen killing young, and there is one record of a female eating a young male. Marmots do not ordinarily eat flesh, and they do not feed at road kills as ground squirrels sometimes do. Probably infanticide occurs when there is some upset in the otherwise smoothly functioning social system.

A major disadvantage of group living in marmots is that reproduction is inhibited in some of the females. Females in a harem are normally sisters or mother and daughters.

Adult females tend to suppress reproduction by younger females, so that per capita reproductive output declines as harem size increases. It might be advantageous for younger females to leave, but females living singly may be forced to occupy inferior sites. In many birds as well as in social insects, non-reproductive individuals serve as "helpers" in the nest. In families of birds and social insects, helpers obtain genetic representation in the next generation by enhancing the success of superior reproducers that share many of their genes. Despite the fact that marmot family members are closely related and that reproductive suppression does occur, it appears that "unselfish behavior"—the enhancement of the behavior of superior reproducers—does not occur. Adult females compete for resources and the opportunity to reproduce. Yearlings and two-year-olds, of both sexes, must assume submissive roles until they are able to compete successfully.

We admired the marmots that lived around our home, and we admired them more after we had learned more about them. The shrill whistle of a marmot is a sound of the high country as cherished as the scent of conifers and the sight of riotous wildflowers. The lifestyle of marmots may differ from ours, but marmots pose no serious threat to their environment and keep their population size within reasonable limits. Humans might have learned from them, but now it is too late.

19

Insects Beyond Count

HUMANS HAVE A passion for making lists, and we were no exception. In the course of our thirteen years in our mountain home, we listed 117 kinds of birds, some seen only once or twice, others every day. There were twenty-four species of mammals, four snakes, and so far as we know only one amphibian, the chorus frogs that we could hear from our deck on summer evenings. We collected sixty-two species of butterflies, but we suspect that a lepidopterist could have found several more. There were 225 species of predatory wasps (a specialty of ours), two of them new to science. We made no attempt to collect the beetles extensively; there were simply too many of them. A complete survey of all the insects would have taken a lifetime, and we would probably not find all of them.

Why are there so many kinds of insects, even in an area of variable and sometimes very cold climate and of unremarkable terrain? Certainly their small size is a factor; one might find many hundreds of species and many thousands of individuals within the home range of one mountain lion. An herbivorous insect needs only a few leaves, if a leaf miner only one. Scavengers avail themselves of the abundant dung, carcasses, and decaying organic matter that is always present. These are the street cleaners and morticians of the natural world, and we would do well to salute them for their services.

This leaves us with an enormous array of insects that eat other insects, either as predators or parasites. These are highly esteemed by organic gardeners, as they keep pest species under control (though even "good" insects, such as lady beetles, have their parasites). That the natural world maintains a degree of stability is to a considerable extent the result of the "bug eat bug" scenario. Most people, even entomologists, do not appreciate how many insect species live at the expense of other insects, usually herbivores. A single family of parasitic wasps, the Ichneumonidae, includes several tens of thousands of species. There were several hundred species around our home (over and above the predatory wasps mentioned earlier). Yet ichneumons are only one of several large groups of wasps and flies that live at the expense of other insects.

That many pest species thrive on farms and plantations is so well known that the U.S. Department of Agriculture is greatly concerned with the problems they present, and pesticide manufacturers thrive. Current agricultural practices provide unlimited food for specific herbivores and leave the predators and parasites on the sidelines, if not eliminated altogether. Foresters well know that under natural conditions herbivorous insects can sometimes "run rampant" if, for a few years, they are able to build up their populations more rapidly than their natural enemies are able to do.

When we first moved to our mountain home, we found ourselves in the midst of an outbreak of spruce budworms on Douglas-firs. Our picnic table was just beneath an infested tree, and the budworms (attractive caterpillars about an inch long) descended on silken threads from the branches above, unwelcome guests at our lunch. This tree was not seriously defoliated and survived, but on a slope across the valley from our house a great many Douglas-firs were killed, as they were in many parts of the Rockies. It was several years before the dead trees began to be replaced by new ones. Western spruce budworms occur in many parts of the West and attack true firs and spruces as well as Douglas-firs. They are not appreciated by the lumber industry or by persons who simply enjoy mountain forests (that is, everyone).

Since it was obvious that spruce budworms had far out-paced their parasites, it seemed a good opportunity to find out what the parasites might be. So we collected quite a few mature caterpillars and reared them through the pupal stage to produce delicate, mottled, orange-brown moths, which in nature would have flown off to lay their eggs on Douglas-fir buds. On two successive years ten percent produced not moths but tachina flies of a species well known to be a para-site of the budworms, one of some forty species known to attack them. Presumably these and other parasites would have soon "caught up" with the budworms, which in fact were already in decline by this time.

A more interesting bit of information arose serendipi-tously. We had been "trap-nesting" for predatory wasps around our house to see what species occurred there. Trap nests are made of pieces of pine about six inches long and an inch square, with a hole bored in one end, simulating the beetle borings in which certain wasps usually nest. Eleven of our trap nests were occupied by a wasp that stocked the burrows with paralyzed caterpillars in cells separated by mud partitions. (The fact that we kept a bird bath probably helped the wasps make mud in this very dry environment.) The eleven nests contained 270 small caterpillars, of which 7 percent were budworms. However, some of the nests were stocked after the budworms had completed their development. Of four nests provisioned while the bud-worms were still active, 24 percent of the caterpillars were budworms. In places suitable for nesting by these wasps, they might have considerable impact on spruce budworm populations.

One other trap nest contained a surprise. It held a single paralyzed budworm that bore twenty tiny eggs—a remarkable number, as most wasps place a single egg on their prey. The eggs produced larvae that rapidly consumed the caterpillar and spun silken cocoons only five days later. Sixteen days from the time of the initial discovery, several very small female wasps emerged from the cocoons. We identified the wasps as *Goniozus gracilicornis*, a formidable name for a wasp three millimeters long (about an eighth of an inch). Members of this group (Bethylidae) are unique in laying several eggs on their relatively large prey, most of the eggs producing females. This is a very economical arrangement, since one male can fertilize several of his sisters, and inbreeding seems no deterrent to these wasps. Probably a male or two had emerged from our cocoons and had escaped from our rearing cage, something these tiny insects are adept at doing.

Although this species of wasp had not previously been recorded as a predator on spruce budworms, the real surprise was that the wasp managed to carry a caterpillar about eight times its own length, and many times its own weight, into the trap nest. The trap had been tied to the branch of a pine about four feet high. The wasp must have found the caterpillar on a nearby Douglas-fir, or on the ground beneath it, and carried it over the ground and up the trunk of the pine to the trap nest. How it accomplished this is one of those dramas that must occur in nature frequently, unseen by human eyes.

A decade or two before we moved to our mountain home there had been another massive attack by an insect that had evidently outpaced its natural enemies. This was the mountain pine beetle, a cylindrical beetle no more than a quarter of an inch long that attacks ponderosas and other pine trees. The female beetles make long tunnels beneath bark, then lay eggs in niches along the sides of the burrow. The eggs hatch to produce tiny grubs that work their way perpendicularly to the original burrow. The resulting engraving on the wood can be deadly to the pine tree if repeated many times and if accompanied by an invasion of blue-stain fungus. Pine trees resist invasion by producing pitch at the point of beetle entry, but when the beetles arrive *en masse* they overwhelm the trees' defenses.

When we moved to the mountains we found many pine trees that had been killed and had fallen to the ground, the aftermath of a major epidemic of pine beetles. Such widespread death of trees, either from pine beetles or spruce budworms, has major effects on all plants and animals living there. Grasses and wildflowers grow in places once shaded; bushes proliferate, providing more browse for deer; woodpeckers flourish on the beetles in dying timber, making holes where bluebirds may nest; field mice, voles, and chipmunks find new places to hide or nest. Trees that are gone are in time replaced by new trees, usually of the same kind but sometimes by aspens.

When we came upon the scene, the pines were healthy and the Douglas-firs that had survived the budworms were doing well; and there were many young trees. But both trees have a great many natural enemies. The U.S. Forest Service's book *Western Forest Insects* lists nearly two hundred insect species known to attack ponderosa pines (one of which we met in the chapter on butterflies, the pine white). The same book lists an even larger number of insects known to attack Douglas-firs. Most of these insects have their own natural enemies: various parasitic wasps and flies as well as predators: insectan, avian, and mammalian. The view of a healthy forest is a pleasing one, not only aesthetically but philosophically: however apparently tranquil, there is a great deal going on, most of it on a size level and a time scale not readily grasped by an animal so large and so committed to quick actions as ourselves.

We had an experience with the fate of a more conspicuous herbivore when one year we found some large, showy caterpillars defoliating the squaw currants around our house. Since we had never seen these caterpillars before, we put several in a rearing cage, where they spun large, silken cocoons that later gave rise to beautiful agapema silk moths. Despite its striking appearance, the species had never been reported from this part of the Rockies before. We also reared several parasitic tachina flies. The following summer the caterpillars were less plentiful, and every one we could find bore the white eggs of tachina flies. The next summer we found no caterpillars at all and assumed that the parasites had eliminated them. Four years later they did reappear in numbers, so a few must have survived somewhere, and for the moment they were "ahead of their parasites."

There are three interrelated answers, we think, to the question of why there are so many insects. Small size is certainly one, since many insects are able to share a small piece of the environment, say a bush, a rotting log, or a small stream. Further, most insects are picky eaters; most herbivores are restricted to one type of plant, while most parasites and many predators attack one particular type of prey. So to a considerable extent they share, rather than compete for, the available resources. Finally, populations of all insects are suppressed by parasites and predators (as well as climate), so that only occasionally do they build up populations that overwhelm their environments.

The few thousands of insect species that lived around our home represented only a tiny fraction of the world's total, which may exceed two million, most living in warmer parts of the globe. That there are so many species, and that some attain huge population sizes, at least now and then, provides endless opportunities for research by entomologists and by people who are simply curious. Unfortunately many people are unaware of or indifferent to the insect life around them, or are simply "bug haters." They are missing a great deal. Insects are not only fun to study, but they play a major role in our world, and understanding them, as best we can, is essential to our own well being.

20

Afterword

OUR DECISION TO MOVE from the mountains was a difficult one. Our reasons were personal, but in a sense they copied an historic change, from the time when people lived in clean air, close to nature, to our modern urbanized society, where nature is seen as space for houses, businesses, malls, golf courses, ski lifts, and landfills. So long as space is needed for more people, and so long as the acquisition of material goods is our major obsession, there is no way of reversing the trend.

In his book *The End of Nature*, Bill McKibben maintains that "nature, the independent force that has surrounded us since our earliest days, cannot coexist with our numbers and our habits." Already we have filled the atmosphere with greenhouse gases and other pollutants, reduced the protective ozone layer, and begun to alter living things through biotechnology. We may well be able to create a world that supports our numbers and our habits, says McKibben, but "it will be an artificial world, a space station." Elsewhere: "There is no future in loving nature."

To us, it seems undeniable that we are far along in creating such an artificial world. Efforts to check human population growth are thwarted at every turn, and the mass media forever cry "consume, consume." We ourselves grieve for the plants and animals that are being displaced or eliminated, but such grief is far from common. And we wonder if the current extinction rate of species throughout the world (perhaps three every *hour*, according to Edward O. Wilson) is not unbecoming of a society that not only pretends to practice love and compassion but may someday need some of those lost species urgently. "Each species," writes Wilson, "is a masterpiece of evolution, offering a vast source of useful scientific knowledge because it is so thoroughly adapted to the environment in which it lives." Ought we to be so cavalier in our destruction of the natural world? No doubt some of us will go on loving nature even if there is "no future in it." But we see nothing in our politics, local, national, or international, least of all in society's diverse religions, that encourages us to believe that a reversal of present trends is possible. We are not doomsayers, since we recognize that a wholly artificial world will supply people with the thrills and comforts they enjoy, so long as there is room to move about and enough resources to sustain us.

Persons who feel that the end of nature is something that should be prevented, or at least mitigated, have a difficult task of persuasion. All who have thought about the matter have concluded that only a new, universal way of thinking, a new ethic, will be required. As Wilson puts it in his thoughtful book *Consilience*, our choice is "whether to accept our corrosive and risky behavior as the unavoidable price of population and economic growth, or to take stock of ourselves and search for a new environmental ethic."

There is no shortage of books on bioethics, but few have made it to the mass market, flooded as it is with books extolling our current way of life in one way or another, or a future that leaves no room for nature. That we were born of nature and have depended upon the natural world for succor through history no longer seems relevant. Even among ourselves, we constantly violate our nebulous ethical codes.

Is there hope of extending ethics to plants, animals, or ecosystems?

No doubt coral-root orchids still bloom along our trail, bumblebees still bumble from flower to flower in meadows we used to roam, and squirrels and crossbills still harvest seeds from the pines. Nature, for them, is the world; they are utterly dependent upon one another and upon the soil and the rain. May they do well, so long as we permit them the space to live and multiply. If their environment disappears, it will not be their doing—but it will be their undoing.

References

Chapter One

Evans, H.E., and M.A. Evans. 1991. *Cache la Poudre: The Natural History of a Rocky Mountain River.* University Press of Colorado.
Mutel, C.F., and J.C. Emerick. 1984. *From Grassland to Glacier: The Natural History of Colorado.* Johnson Books.

Chapter Two

Herbers, J.M. 1979. Caste-biased polyethism in a mound-building ant species. In *American Midland Naturalist,* 101: 69–75.
Talbot, M. 1972. Flights and swarms of the ant *Formica obscuripes* Forel. In *Journal of the Kansas Entomological Society,* 45: 254–258.
Weber, N. 1935. The biology of the thatching ant, *Formica rufa obscuripes* Forel in North America. In *Ecological Monographs,* 5: 167–206.

Chapter Three

Calder, W. 1998. Migration of the rufous hummingbird. In *Nature Conservancy,* March/April 1998.
Miller, S.J., and D.W. Inouye. 1983. Roles of the wing whistle in the territorial behaviour of the male broad-tailed hummingbird (*Selasphorus platycercus*). In *Animal Behavior,* 31: 689–700.
Skutch, A. 1973. *The Life of the Hummingbird.* Crown Publishers.
Skutch, A. 1980. *A Naturalist on a Tropical Farm.* University of California Press.

Chapter Four

Dethier, V.G. 1980. *The World of the Tent-Makers.* University of Massachusetts Press.
Evans, H.E. 1987. Observations on the prey and nests of *Podalonia occidentalis* Murray. In *Pan-Pacific Entomologist,* 63: 130–134.
Newcomer, E.J. 1930. Notes on the habits of a digger wasp and its inquiline flies. In *Annals of the Entomological Society of America,* 23: 552–563.

O'Neill, K.M., and H.E. Evans. 1999. Observations on the prey and nest clusters of *Podalonia valida* (Cresson). In *Proceedings of the Entomological Society of Washington*, 101: 312–315.

Chapter Five

Everett, M. 1977. *A Natural History of Owls*. Hamlyn Publishing Group.

Heinrich, B. 1987. *One Man's Owl*. Princeton University Press.

Wilkinson, C.F. 1992. *Crossing the Next Meridian: Land, Water, and the Future of the West*. Island Press.

Chapter Six

Fye, R.E., and Medler, J.T. 1954. Field domiciles for bumblebees. In *Journal of Economic Entomology*, 47: 672–676.

Heinrich, B. 1979. *Bumblebee Economics*. Harvard University Press.

Heinrich, B. 1996. *The Thermal Warriors: Strategies of Insect Survival*. Harvard University Press.

O'Neill, K.M., H.E. Evans, and L.B. Bjostad. Territorial behaviour in males of three species of North American bumblebees. In *Canadian Journal of Zoology*, 69: 604–613.

Chapter Seven

Belles-Isles, J.C., and J. Picman. 1986. House wren nest-destroying behavior. In *The Condor*, 88: 190–193.

Johnson, L.S., and L.H. Kermott. 1991. Effect of nest-site supplementation on polygynous behavior in the house wren. In *The Condor*, 93: 784–787.

Kroodsma, D.E. 1977. Correlates of song organization among North American wrens. In *American Naturalist*, 111: 995–1008.

Searcy, W.A., and M. Andersson. 1986. Sexual selection and the evolution of song. In *Annual Review of Ecology and Systematics*, 17: 507–533.

Chapter Eight

Bowers, M.D. 1983. The role of iridoid glycosides in host-plant specificity of checkerspot butterflies. In *Journal of Chemical Ecology*, 9: 475–493.

Pierce, N.E., and P.S. Mead. 1981. Parasitoids as selective agents in the symbiosis between lycaenid butterfly larvae and ants. In *Science*, 211: 1185–1187.

Chapter Nine

Armstrong, D.M. 1987. *Rocky Mountain Mammals*. Colorado Associated University Press.
Farentinos, R.C. 1972. Social dominance and mating activity in the tassel-eared squirrel (*Sciurus aberti ferreus*). In *Animal Behavior*, 20: 316–326.
Snyder, M.A., and Y.B. Linhart. 1993. Barking up the Right Tree. In *Natural History*, no. 9, 1993.

Chapter Ten

Evans, H.E. 1988. Observations on swarms of *Rhamphomyia sociabilis* (Williston). In *Journal of the New York Entomological Society*, 96: 316–322.
Funk, D.H., and D.W. Tallamy. 2000. Courtship role reversal and deceptive signals in the long-tailed dance fly, *Rhamphomyia longicauda*. In *Animal Behaviour*, 59: 411-421.
Svensson, B.G. 1997. Swarming behavior, sexual dimorphism, and female reproductive states in the sex role-reversed dance fly species *Rhamphomyia marginata*. In *Journal of Insect Behavior*, 10: 783–804.
Thornhill, R. 1980. Sexual selection in the black-tipped hangingfly. In *Scientific American*, 242(6): 162–172.

Chapter Eleven

Egoscue, H.J. 1962. The bushy-tailed wood rat: a laboratory colony. In *Journal of Mammalogy*, 43: 328–337.
Finley, R.B., Jr. 1958. The Wood Rats of Colorado. In *University of Kansas Publications, Museum of Natural History*, 10: 213–552.
Horne, E.A., M. McDonald, and O.J. Reichman, 1998. Changes in the cache contents over winter in artificial dens of the eastern woodrat. In *Journal of Mammalogy*, 79: 898–905.

Chapter Twelve

Evans, H.E. 1989. The mating and predatory behavior of *Mellinus rufin-odus* Cresson. In *Pan-Pacific Entomologist*, 65: 414–417.

Hamm, A.H., and O.W. Richards. 1930. The biology of the British fosso-rial wasps ... In *Transactions of the Entomological Society of London*, 78: 95–131.

Chapter Thirteen

Kamil, A.C., and J.E. Jones. 1997. The seed-storing corvid Clark's nut-cracker learns geometric relationships among landmarks. In *Nature* (London), 390: 276–278.

Tomback, D.F. 1980. How nutcrackers find their seed stores. In *The Condor*, 82: 10–19.

Vander Wall, S.B. 1990. *Food Hoarding in Animals*. University of Chicago Press.

Chapter Fourteen

Gess, S.K. 1996. *The Pollen Wasps: Ecology and Natural History of the Masarinae*. Harvard University Press.

Longair, R.W. 1987. Mating behavior at floral resources in two species of *Pseudomasaris*. In *Proceedings of the Entomological Society of Washington*, 89: 759–769.

Chapter Fifteen

Benkman, C.W. 1993. Adaptation to single resources and the evolution of crossbill (*Loxia*) diversity. In *Ecological Monographs*, 63: 305–325.

Benkman, C.W., and A.K. Lindholm. 1991. The advantages and evolution of a morphological novelty. In *Nature* (London), 349: 519–520.

Chapter Sixteen

Evans, H.E. 1993. Observations on aggregations of males of two species of beewolves. In *Psyche*, 100: 25–33.

Evans, H.E., and K.M. O'Neill. 1988. *The Natural History and Behavior of North American Beewolves*. Cornell University Press.

Chapter Seventeen

Harrington, H.D. 1967. *Edible Native Plants of the Rocky Mountains.* University of New Mexico Press.

Weber, W.A. 1972. *Rocky Mountain Flora.* Colorado Associated University Press.

Chapter Eighteen

Armitage, K.M. 1991. Social and population dynamics of yellow-bellied marmots: results from long-term research. In *Annual Review of Ecology and Systematics*, 22: 379–407.

Armitage, K.M. 1998. Reproductive strategies of yellow-bellied marmots: energy conservation and differences between the sexes. In *Journal of Mammalogy*, 79: 385–393.

Shriner, W.M. 1998. Yellow-bellied marmot and golden-mantled ground squirrel responses to heterospecific alarm calls. In *Animal Behavior*, 55: 529–536.

Waring, G.H. 1966. Sounds and communications of the yellow-bellied marmot (*Marmota flaviventris*). In *Animal Behavior*, 14: 177–183.

Chapter Nineteen

Evans, H.E. 1987. Observations on natural enemies of western spruce budworm (*Choristoneura occidentalis* Freeman) in the Rocky Mountain area. In *Great Basin Naturalist*, 47: 319–321.

Furniss, R.L., and V.M. Carolin. 1977. Western Forest Insects. In United States Department of Agriculture, Forest Service, Miscellaneous Publication no. 1339.

Chapter Twenty

McKibben, B. 1989. *The End of Nature.* Random House.

Wilson, E.O. 1998. *Consilience.* Alfred A. Knopf.